COPYCAT RECIPES

HOW TO MAKE YOUR FAVORITE DISHES AT HOME: DELICIOUS MEALS FROM MEAT TO DESSERTS. COOK THE MOST POPULAR RECIPES AND SHARE WITH YOUR FAMILY.

By

Matt Barrel

TABLE OF CONTENTS

INTRODUCTION

Meals at the restaurant are the greatest. We always eat in our favorite restaurants, but it's sometimes hard to drink the motivation to leave home comforts and invest $15 on dinner. This is why we are pleased that a number of meals from our favorite chains (guilty fast food, and so on) were recreated there by food bloggers and other great chefs. You may thank these geniuses for enabling you to whip up anything you want and eat while you were lazy on your own couch.

Whether you are fascinated with the food, or unconsciously addicted to P.F. Chang's Mongolian Pork, presumably for it there's a copycat version. What enhances it is that they sometimes even have a way to make the food better — and you can know it is created from fresh ingredients.

The pleasures of sharing a home-cooked meal

Cooking helps together families and home cooking is a great way for your family to get together over the dining table. Everyone enjoys a home-cooked meal— particularly moody teens and chicken eaters. And if you stay home, that's not preparing, or dining either. Sharing meals with others is a great way to broaden the social network. Getting thankful feedback on a meal that you prepared for someone may also give your self-esteem a real boost.

Consider your meals a shared activity. The simple act of talking to a friend or a lover at the table will play an important role in alleviating tension and improving mood. Gather the kids together and keep up with each other's everyday life. Invite a relative, partner or neighbour if you stay alone.

Turn the displays off. Please stop at the Television, turn off your cell and remove any disruptions, so you can really listen to the person with whom you share a meal. You can also prevent overcrowding by minimizing phones and dining with others.

Eat with others. Fish with others. Invite your spouse, coworker or friend to share the responsibility for shopping and cooking—for example, you prepare your entry, the other dessert. Cooking with others can be a fun way to improve your partnerships and sharing expenses can make both of you healthier.

Overcoming obstacles to cooking at home

Despite all the benefits, a lot of us still consider preparing meals as a task, either something that we don't have time for, or something that's only appropriate for experienced cooks. Possibly you've tried cooking prior to and didn't like the end results, or perhaps your kids simply choose takeout food?

Conquering challenges to cooking in the house frequently begins with changing the way you view meal preparation or time invested in the kitchen. Some typical reasons that we do not prepare in the house, and what to do about them, include:

Obstacle 1: "I do not have the time to prepare."
Sure, shopping, chopping active ingredients, cooking, and after that tidying up later on can be time-consuming. But there are plenty of methods to speed things up:
Shop online and have all the components delivered to your door.
Get loved ones included. Trade off shopping and cleanup tasks with your spouse or a next-door neighbor.
Rather than watching cooking programs on the couch, move the TELEVISION into the kitchen and follow along.
Multitask: chat on the phone or watch TV while you cook.
Purchase pre-washed bags of sliced veggies and throw whatever into a crockery pot or cleaner for a healthier meal in no time.
Try a cook-at-home delivery service where the recipes and active ingredients get here on your doorstep.
Do some of the preparation ahead of time. Chop vegetables over the weekend when you're less pressed, for instance, to minimize your last cooking time.
Use fresh components. Salads and raw food dishes can take simply minutes to prepare.

View cooking meals as an enjoyable, relaxing experience rather than a task-- it will not seem nearly as lengthy.

Obstacle 2: "It's less expensive to consume junk food."
A research study from the University of Washington School of Public Health exposed that people who cook at home tend to have much healthier overall diet plans without higher food costs. Another study found that frequent home cooks spent about $60 per month less on food than those who consumed out more often.

Obstacle 3: "I'm too tired to cook at the end of a busy day."
Creating healthy meals does not have to involve a substantial investment of effort.
Packing a slow cooker with meat and vegetables in the early morning enables you to come home to a piping hot meal in the evening, with very little preparation and little cleanup.
When you don't have the time or energy to cook, make meals in bulk and freeze leftovers in single portions to eat.
By cooking your primary protein as soon as a week, such as a roast chicken or slow prepared turkey breasts, you can use the meat to develop simple and fast meals throughout the week, such as soup, salads, sandwiches, burritos, or pasta meals.

Obstacle 4: "I do not know how to cook"
If you're intimidated by the prospect of preparing a home-cooked meal, it's important to remember that cooking is not a precise science.
It's normally perfectly OK to skip an ingredient or replace one thing for another.
Look online or purchase a basic cookbook for simple dish ideas. Similar to anything, the more you cook, the much better you'll become. Even if you're a complete newbie in the kitchen, you'll quickly master some quick, healthy meals.

Obstacle 5: "I hate remaining in the kitchen."

If you hate the concept of spending quality time in the kitchen, you require to embrace your fun side. Cooking is not work, it's recreation!

Play your favorite music, put yourself a glass of wine, and dance around as you slice and peel.

Or listen to an audiobook and lose yourself in an excellent story.

Obstacle 6: "Even if I prepare a well balanced meal in your home, I can't get my household to consume it."

With time, you can wean your family (and yourself) off the taste of takeout and packaged food.

Start small, cooking simply once or twice a week to offer everybody's taste buds a chance to adjust.

Young children enjoy to cook and discover it fun to eat what they've helped to make.

The youth impulse to imitate is strong, so the more your kids see you eating healthy food, the most likely they are to do the same.

Tips for getting started

Begin with healthy, fresh ingredients. The baking of succulent therapies like brownies, cakes and cookies will not improve your wellbeing or waistline. Likewise, consuming too much sugar or salt will make a healthy, nutritious meal unsafe. To ensure your food is good for you and delicious, start with healthy ingredients and taste spices instead of sugar or salt.

Keep it simple. Keep it simple. Steam or bake some tomatoes, barbecue some chicken or fish, incorporate some herbs, seasoning, or balanced sauce. Easy cooking can be delicious and quick.

Cook enough for the remaining. It's nice to have residues for a quick and easy lunch or dinner the next day. Prepare at least twice the quantity you need when you make things like rice or pasta and put it in the fridge for use with certain meals. Freezing remains can also ensure that you have a homemade meal on hand when you don't feel like cooking.

Make healthier product substitutions, instead of baking, barbecue or roast. Replace garlic or onion powder with oil. Cut the sugar needed by 1/3 to 1/2 in most recipes. Reduce meat and increase in stews and casseroles vegetables. Select whole grain pasta and bread varieties and substitute a wheat meal with a white bleached meal as you bake.

Stock up on basics. Basics. You should typically use essentials of products such as corn, noodles, olive oil, nuts, wheat, and stock cubes daily. Holding in hand tuna tins, carrots, tomatoes and bags of frozen veggies can be useful when you are pushed for time in rapidly mixing meals.

Offer any leeway to yourself. It's all right to roast rice or steam vegetables over. It'll be smoother, quicker and taster after a couple of attempts!

Benefits of Cooking At Home

Scratch cooked recipes are always the greatest. Many people assume, however, that lots of time and product expertise are needed. Many are excluded from cooking and rely on pre-cooked or drinking meals. Not all products are made in the same way when it comes to healthy options.

For apps that allow you to order only a few taps, cooking dinner can be incredibly tenting. However, trade-offs often exist for convenience.

Meals in the restaurant can contain several unhealthy ingredients. There is also much more than what you lack when you feed from a take-outs.

Here are a few explanations why you should consider having your own cooking dinner tonight!

A Nutrient-Dense Plate

If prepared food arrives from outside the home you typically have limited knowledge about salt, sugar and processed oils. For fact, we also apply more to our meal when it is served to the table. You will say how much salt, sugar and oil is being used as you prepare meals at home.

Creativity often happens when you cook at home, and you can attach a range of plant foods to a variety of colours. You are not only acquiring kilograms, antioxidants, minerals and phytonutrients, but also introducing nice textures and colors to your meals. You would be shocked by how much food in a single dish is collected.

Portion control from home can also be regulated. When food is cooked for us, we tend to eat all or most of it. Try to use little dishes at home, but ensure that all good things like vegetables, fruits, whole grains and legumes are filled. You're certainly going to be satisfied and happy.

Increased Fruit and Vegetable Intake

The typical western diet loses both the weight and durability of plant foods we need to preserve. Many People eat only two servings of fresh fruit and vegetables a day, while at least 5 portions are required. Tons of pre-made food, like restaurant food goods, restrict fruit and vegetable parts.

By supplying you with the convenience of cooking at home, you have complete control over the food you consume. The message to note is that your attention will continue with the intake of more fruit and vegetables. Attach them to your cooking, snack them, or exchange them with your relatives on their way. Then take steps towards organic alternatives. Also, it is always better to eat entire fruits and vegetables, whether or not organic, than processed foods.

Save Money and Use What You Have

Just because you haven't visited your local health food or food store this week doesn't mean you get stuck with taking in. Open your cupboard and fridge and see what you can make for a meal. It can be as easy as gluten-free rice, roasted tomatoes, carrots, frozen vegetables and lemon juice. This simple meal is packed with fiber, protein, vitamins and minerals. Best of all, in less than 30 minutes, it is delicious and can be prepared. It saves you money in the long run and allows you sufficient food to share with or to have a break the next day.

Sensible Snacking

Bringing premade snacks saves time, but everything goes back to what's in these products still. You don't have to give up your favorite treats, but there is a way to make them more nutritious and often taste better. Swap your chips and dip the chopped vegetables into hummus. Create your own snacks with bagged potato chips or carrots. Take a bowl and make your own popcorn on top of your stove or in the popcorn machine. You can control the amount of salt, sugar and oil added.

Share Your Delicious Health
Once you make your own recipes, you are so proud of your achievements. Furthermore, the food tastes amazing. Don't confuse me now–some of your inventive recipes won't taste the same thing, but your cuisine will be loved by friends and family with constant practice and experimentation. You will see them enjoy the best nutritious food because of you and your faith in spreading health and love.

It gives you a chance to reconnect
Cooking together can give you a chance to reconnect with your partner and your loved ones. Cooking also has other benefits. The American Psychological Association says that working together with new things — like learning a new recipe— can help maintain a relationship between a pair.

It's proven to be healthier
Many research Trusted Source say that those who eat more often than not have a healthier diet overall. Such studies also show that in restaurants menus, salt, saturated fat, total fat, and average calories are typically higher than in-house diets.
You have complete control over what is in your food whether you put fresh products together or shipped them straight to your door using a company like Plated. This can make a difference in your overall health.

It's easier to watch your calories
The average fast food order is between 1,100 and 1,200 calories in total–nearly all the recommended daily calorie intake (1,600 to 2,400 calories) by a woman and almost two thirds (2,000 to 3,000 calories) by a man daily. So think again if you felt the independent restaurants so smaller chains would do well. Such products suck up an average of 1.327 calories per meal of additional calories.

Creating your own food ensures you can guarantee that the portion sizes and calories are where you want them. Recipes also come with nutritional information and tips for sizing, which ease this.

It's a time saver
Part of shopping is to wait for food to come or travel to get it. It may take much more time, depending on where you live, on what time you order, and whether or not the delivery person is good at directions!
It doesn't have to take much time to cook at home if you don't want it. You remove the need to search ingredients or foodstuffs by using a service like Plated. Everything you need is at your house, in the exact amount that you use.

It can be a money saver, too
In the long run, home-cooked food will save you money. A collection of basic ingredients also arrives at a lower price than a single dish. You can also consume more of a meal at home than if you buy a take-out or take a rest to work the next day. After a couple of weeks, you will see big savings starting to add up.

It's personalized
Cooking at home gives you the chance to enjoy the food you want, how you like it. For starters, with Plated, if you want your meat more well-done or less sweet, the formula includes suggested changes.

Cutting Costs

Nobody has to remind you that it's pricey to eat out. The disparity between a local restaurant sandwich and a kitchen sandwich is more than a feeling. The purchasing of packaged food in a restaurant typically costs far more than the buying of your own products. Cooking at home helps you to get more for your money by raising the excess expenses of cooking and servicing restaurants. The more often you make your own food, the more money you save.

Enjoying the Process

Once you come back home from a busy day, there is little more enjoyable than disconnecting from work emails, voicemails, unfinished assignments or homework. Cooking at home presents you with a break from your routine and space for imagination. Rather than listen to noisy messages, you should put on the radio, collect spices and reflect on the odors that sizzle on the stove or roast vegetables. You may be shocked by how much you like when you make a daily habit of preparing food.

If your breakfast is great, lunch soup or fresh tomato sauce for dinner, home cooking is a worthy investment. In return for your time and energy in preparation, you will benefit richly— from cost savings to fun with friends.

And the more time you spend in the oven, the more you get to make fantastic food!

Try Plated

Ready to download and cook your smartphone? Plated is a meal kit delivery service that offers all the above and more positive features!

Choose from a weekly menu of designed recipes and get all you need right at your door. Pre-portioned foods are of the highest quality only and contain fresh, seasonal, organical and sustainable seafood items and hormone-free meat.

Recipes vary from meals that require just 30 minutes to prepare, to food that is as demanding as it rewardes. What they all say is that they find dinner a delight to consume and cook.

Things needed to be a great home cook

An efficient kitchen area personnel runs rapidly, quietly, and keeps up with the dance. Below is a list of some of their secrets that will benefit any house cook.

1. Master mise en location.
What it implies to a chef? Before you prepare, have actually whatever determined, peeled, chopped, pans greased, and so on and within reach.

2. A sharp knife is essential.
Hone it regularly and focus on honing. Dull knives threaten and make cutting much more tough.

3. Taste as you go.
Often a little more salt or a dash of spice brings excellence. Salt as you go.
Don't be afraid of salt! Given that you're preparing a fresh meal instead of consuming a packaged one, you're beginning with much less salt to begin with.

5. But lose the salt shaker.
Use a little bowl of kosher salt and include pinches as you prepare and taste. It's simpler to control the quantity and makes sure even coverage.

6. Tongs are an extension of your hand.

Walk into any restaurant kitchen and you'll see a set of tongs in almost every cook's hand-- generally gripped low down on the manage for optimum control. Use it to turn meat, pull work out of the oven, stabilize a steak while slicing, the list goes on and on.

7. Put a wet paper towel under a cutting board.

Not just are cutting boards that move on the counter annoying, they're very unsafe when you're trying and holding a knife to slice something. Wet a paper towel and lay it under the board and it will not budge!

8. Burn chicken breast and surface in the oven.

Chefs scorch a piece of meat, poultry, or fish in a pan and then place it in the oven. Not just does this free up burners, it leads to a much moister outcome.

9. Do not overcrowd your pan.

When browning or roasting anything, the propensity is to stuff as much in the pan as possible-- resist! Do it in smaller batches instead. Crowding the pan leads to steaming and lowers the temperature level of the pan so you will not get the caramelization you're trying to find-- which's where the flavor is.

10. Prepare with a 1:1 ratio of butter and oil.

Oil stops the butter from burning and the butter includes richness to the dish.

11. Cut completions off onions, tomatoes, cantaloupe, etc

. Basically do this for any other food that does not remain stable on the cutting board to make a flat surface area. This permits you to have total control of the product as you chop.

12. When baking, only mix up until all components are included.
Over-mixing causes strength by developing the gluten in the flour. For light and fluffy cupcakes, just mix till the batter's come together.

13. Your broiler is generally an upside down grill.
Utilize it for more than storage!

14. Don't forget the power of your nose.
Check on it if something in the oven smells done but the timer's still ticking.

15. Tidy as you go.
This easy pointer makes a world of difference. Wipe down your cutting board in between products. Not only is it difficult to slice something that is swimming in tomato juices, but it's also hazardous to slice on a wet surface area.

Best Restaurant Copycat Recipes

5 Ingredient Peanut Butter Cookies

Active ingredients
1 cup creamy peanut butter
1/2 cup granulated sugar
1/2 cup brown sugar
1 large egg
1 teaspoon vanilla extract

Instructions
Preheat oven to 350 °. Line a large baking sheet with a silicone baking mat or parchment paper. Set aside.

In the bowl of a stand mixer or in a large bowl with a hand mixer, beat the peanut butter, white sugar, and brown sugar together on high up until smooth and velvety, 2-3 minutes. Add the egg and vanilla and mix up until combined.

Utilizing a heaping tablespoon, spoon the dough and roll into 1 1/4- inch balls. Put on ready cookie sheet and place roughly 2-3 inches apart. Utilize a fork to push the cookies down, creating a cross-hatch pattern.

Bake in the preheated 350 degree oven for about 8 minutes.

Enable cookies to finish cooling entirely on baking sheet prior to removing. Shop in an airtight container.

Cheesy Spinach Artichoke Dip

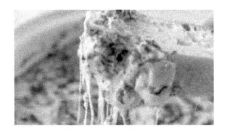

Active ingredients
8 ounces cream cheese softened
1/4 cup mayo
1/2 cup grated Parmesan cheese
1 clove garlic minced and peeled
1/2 teaspoon dried basil
1/4 teaspoon salt
1/4 teaspoon black pepper
14 ounces artichoke hearts chopped and drained
10 ounces frozen chopped spinach defrosted and drained
Shredded mozzarella cheese

Instructions
Preheat oven to 350 degrees F. Lightly grease a little baking meal.

In a medium bowl, mix together cream cheese, mayo, Parmesan cheese, garlic, pepper, basil, and salt. Gently stir in artichoke hearts and spinach.

Transfer the mixture to the prepared baking dish. Leading with mozzarella cheese. Bake in the preheated oven 25 minutes, until bubbly and lightly browned.

Nutrition
Calcium: 206mg

Best Homemade Sloppy Joes

Active ingredients
1 pound lean ground beef
1 medium onion diced
1 medium green bell pepper diced
2 ribs celery diced
1 (8 ounce) can tomato sauce
1 (6 ounce) can tomato paste
2 tablespoons Worcestershire sauce
4 cloves garlic crushed
1 tablespoon brown sugar
1 teaspoon salt
1 teaspoon ground mustard
1/2 teaspoon crushed red pepper flakes
8 hamburger buns

Instructions
In a large frying pan over medium-high heat, cook ground beef and yellow onion together, stirring periodically, till beef is browned and cooked through.

Drain pipes any excess fat from the frying pan and return skillet to heat.

Include bell pepper, celery, tomato sauce, tomato paste, Worcestershire sauce, garlic, brown sugar, salt, ground mustard, and red pepper flakes. Stir to integrate.

Give a simmer and decrease heat to medium low. Simmer for 15 to 30 minutes. Simmering time depends upon how crisp you want the veggies.
Serve meat hot on toasted buns.

Notes
You can change the amount of vegetables to your own personal taste. However, the veggies add extra taste and amazing texture to this traditionally mushy sandwich of our childhood, and we do recommend adhering to the recipe as carefully as possible.

Nutrition
Salt: 598mg

Finest Ever Bran Muffins

Active ingredients
1 1/2 cups 100% all bran cereal.
1 cup buttermilk.
1/3 cup coconut oil melted.
1 big egg.
2/3 cup brown sugar.
1/2 teaspoon vanilla extract.
1 cup all-purpose flour.
1 teaspoon baking soda.
1 teaspoon baking powder.
1/2 teaspoon salt.

Instructions
Preheat oven to 450 degrees Fahrenheit. Lightly spray a muffin pan with nonstick spray or line with paper cups.

In a medium sized mixing bowl soak bran cereal and buttermilk for about 10 minutes up until it gets all soggy.

Include melted coconut oil, egg, brown sugar, vanilla extract, flour, baking soda, baking powder and salt. Stir completely. This mix will be very thick.

Divide the batter similarly amongst the 12 muffin cups, filling practically all the way full.

Bake in the preheated 450 degree oven for 5 minutes. Without opening the door, decrease the heat to 350 degrees and let the muffins continue baking another 8 to 10 minutes. Eliminate from the pan and cool on a wire rack.

Copycat Texas Roadhouse Rolls with Cinnamon-Honey Butter

Active ingredients

1/2 cup warm water (100 ° F to
110 ° F). 1(1/4 oz.) envelope active dry yeast.
1/4 cup plus 1 tsp. granulated sugar, divided.
3/4 cup (6 oz.) salted butter, softened and divided.
1 cup whole milk, warmed.
2 big eggs, beaten.
1 teaspoon kosher salt.
5 cups (21 1/4 oz.) bread flour, plus more for working surface area.
Cooking spray.
1 tablespoon honey.
1/2 teaspoon ground cinnamon.

Instructions

Stir together water, yeast, and 1 teaspoon of the sugar in a small bowl; let stand until foamy, about 5 minutes. Location 1/4 cup of the butter in a little microwavable bowl. Microwave on HIGH up until melted, about 25 seconds.

Integrate melted butter, yeast mixture, milk, eggs, salt, and remaining 1/4 cup sugar in the bowl of an electric mixer fitted with a dough hook. Beat on medium-low up until well integrated, about 10 seconds. With mixer running on medium-low, gradually include flour, beating up until all flour is included. Continue kneading until dough is smooth and elastic, about 4 minutes. (Dough will be sticky.) Transfer to a big lightly greased bowl; cover with plastic wrap; let increase in a warm place (80 ° to 85 °) till doubled in volume, about 1 1/2 hours.

Preheat oven to 375 ° F with racks in leading and lower thirds. Line 2 baking sheets with parchment paper, and gently coat parchment with cooking spray. Turn dough out onto a lightly floured work surface. Gently sprinkle top of dough with flour, and carefully pat into a 14- x 8-inch rectangular shape (about 1/2-inch thick). Cut into 15 (about 2 1/2 -inch) squares; set up on ready baking sheets, leaving 1 1/2- inches in between each square. Cover loosely with plastic wrap; let rise in a warm place (80 ° to 85 °) up until increased in volume, about 30 minutes.

Meanwhile, beat together honey, cinnamon, and staying 1/2 cup butter with electric mixer on medium-high up until well integrated and fluffy, about 2 minutes. Set aside.

Bake rolls in preheated oven up until golden brown, 15 to 18 minutes, rotating pans after 10 minutes. Brush hot rolls lightly with honey butter. Serve warm with staying honey butter.

Bo-Berry Biscuits

Active ingredients
BISCUITS
3 tablespoons unsalted butter, melted, divided
2 cups (about 8 1/2 oz.) self-rising flour, plus more for work surface
1/4 cup granulated sugar
1 teaspoon kosher salt
1/2 cup (4 oz.) unsalted butter, frozen
1 cup freeze-dried blueberries
1 cup buttermilk
GLAZE
2 cups (about 8 oz.) powdered sugar
3 tablespoons fresh lemon juice (from 1 lemon)

Instructions
Prepare the Biscuits: Preheat oven to 475°F. Brush a 10-inch cast-iron skillet with 1 tablespoon of the melted butter.

Whisk together flour, sugar, and salt in a large bowl until combined.

Using a box grater, grate the frozen butter into the flour mixture, and lightly toss to coat butter with flour. Fold blueberries into flour mixture until evenly distributed. Gently stir in buttermilk with a wooden spoon until dough is formed. Do not overmix.

Transfer dough to a lightly floured surface. Lightly sprinkle flour over top of dough. Using a lightly floured rolling pin, roll dough into a 3/4-inch-thick rectangle (about 9 x 5 inches). Fold dough in half so short ends meet. Repeat process 1 more time.

With a floured 2 1/2-inch round cookie cutter, cut out biscuits and place in buttered cast-iron skillet. Use the leftover scraps to make 1 more biscuit, and add to skillet. Bake in preheated oven until tops are golden, about 15 minutes. Brush tops of biscuits with remaining 2 tablespoons melted butter. Let cool 5 minutes in skillet.

Meanwhile, prepare the Glaze: Stir together powdered sugar and lemon juice in a small bowl until smooth. Drizzle glaze on top of biscuits and serve.

Milano Cookies

Active ingredients
1/2 cup (4 oz.) unsalted butter, softened
1/4 cup granulated sugar
1 cup powdered sugar
1/4 teaspoon kosher salt
3 large egg whites
1 tablespoon vanilla extract
1 cup (4 1/4 oz.) all-purpose flour
1/4 cup heavy cream 4 ounces finely chopped semisweet chocolate

Instructions
Preheat oven to 300°F with oven racks in the top and lower third of oven. Beat together butter and granulated sugar in the bowl of a stand mixer on medium speed until well combined, about 1 minute. Gradually add powdered sugar, and beat until smooth, stopping to scrape down sides of bowl as needed. Stir in salt. Add egg whites, 1 at a time, beating well after each addition. Stir in vanilla extract. Gradually add flour, and beat on low speed until batter is smooth, about 30 seconds.
Transfer batter to a piping bag fitted with a 1/4-inch round tip. Pipe 2- x 1-inch ovals (about 36) on 2 baking sheets lined with parchment paper, leaving 1 1/2-inches between each oval. Bake in preheated oven until edges are golden brown, 14 to 18 minutes, rotating pans after 10 minutes. Let cookies cool on baking sheets for 10 minutes. Transfer cookies to a wire rack to cool completely, about 30 minutes.

Meanwhile, microwave cream in a medium microwavable bowl until hot, about 25 seconds. Add chopped chocolate, and stir until smooth. Let stand, stirring occasionally, until mixture has cooled completely and thickened, about 45 minutes.

Transfer chocolate mixture to a piping bag fitted with a 1/4-inch round tip. Pipe about 2 teaspoons mixture onto half of the cookies, leaving a 1/4-inch border. Sandwich with remaining cookies, and press gently to spread filling to edges.

Waffle House Hash Browns

Active ingredients
1 tablespoon melted butter
1 tablespoon canola oil
1 1/2 cups frozen shredded hash browns, partially thawed
2 tablespoons diced onion
1/4 cup diced ham
1 thick American cheese slice

Instructions
Whisk together butter and oil in a small bowl. Reserve 2 teaspoons of butter mixture for later. Heat remaining butter mixture on 1 side of a large nonstick skillet over medium-high. Place hash browns on buttered side of skillet in a round shape about 5 inches wide. Cook, undisturbed, about 5 minutes, until browned and crisp around edges.

Flip hash browns, and cook, undisturbed 4 to 5 more minutes, until other side is browned and crispy. Meanwhile, add reserved butter mixture to other side of skillet; add onion. Cook, stirring often for 2 minutes. Add ham to onion, and cook 2 minutes. Add onions and ham to top of cooked hash browns. Top with cheese slice; turn off heat. Let stand until cheese is melted; serve immediately

Mint Chocolate Milano Cookies

Active ingredients
1/2 cup (4 oz.) unsalted butter, softened
1/4 cup granulated sugar
1 cup powdered sugar
1/4 teaspoon kosher salt
3 large egg whites
1 tablespoon vanilla extract
1 cup (4 1/4 oz.) all-purpose flour
1/4 cup heavy cream
1 (4.67-oz.) pkg. thin crème de menthe chocolate mints, finely chopped

Instructions
Preheat oven to 300°F with oven racks in the top and lower third of oven. Beat together butter and granulated sugar in the bowl of a stand mixer on medium speed until well combined, about 1 minute. Gradually add powdered sugar, and beat until smooth, stopping to scrape down sides of bowl as needed. Stir in salt. Add egg whites, 1 at a time, beating well after each addition. Stir in vanilla extract. Gradually add flour, and beat on low speed until batter is smooth, about 30 seconds.

Transfer batter to a piping bag fitted with a 1/4-inch round tip. Pipe 2- x 1-inch ovals (about 36) on 2 baking sheets lined with parchment paper, leaving 1 1/2-inches between each oval. Bake in preheated oven until edges are golden brown, 14 to 18 minutes, rotating pans after 10 minutes. Let cookies cool on baking sheets for 10 minutes. Transfer cookies to a wire rack to cool completely, about 30 minutes.

Meanwhile, microwave cream in a medium microwavable bowl until hot, about 25 seconds. Add chopped chocolate, and stir until smooth. Let stand, stirring occasionally, until mixture has cooled completely and thickened, about 45 minutes.

Transfer chocolate mixture to a piping bag fitted with a 1/4-inch round tip. Pipe about 2 teaspoons mixture onto half of the cookies, leaving a 1/4-inch border. Sandwich with remaining cookies, and press gently to spread filling to edges.

Panera Bread Mac and Cheese

Active ingredients
1 pound pound dried pasta shells
4 tablespoon unsalted butter
1/4 cup all-purpose flour
2 cups whole milk
1 cup heavy cream
2 teaspoons Dijon mustard
8 ounces (about 2 cups) sharp white cheddar cheese, shredded
4 ounces (about 1 cup) white American cheese, shredded
1 teaspoon kosher salt

Instructions
Cook pasta shells according to package directions; drain well.
In a large pot, melt butter over medium heat; stir in the flour to form a thick paste. Whisk in the milk, heavy cream, and Dijon mustard, whisking until combined.
Add the white cheddar cheese, white American cheese, and salt to pan; stir until melted and combined. Stir in cooked pasta shells. Serve immediately.

Starbucks Pumpkin Scones

Active ingredients
SCONES
2 cups (about 8 1/2 oz.) all-purpose flour
1/3 cup firmly packed light brown sugar
1 tablespoon baking powder
1/2 teaspoon table salt
1/2 teaspoon ground cinnamon
1/4 teaspoon ground ginger
1/4 teaspoon ground nutmeg
1/8 teaspoon ground cloves
1/2 cup (4 oz.) cold butter, cut into 1/2-in. cubes
1/3 cup canned pumpkin puree
2/3 cup plus 2 Tbsp. heavy cream, divided
VANILLA GLAZE
1 cup powdered sugar
3 to 4 tablespoons heavy cream
1/2 teaspoon vanilla extract
PUMPKIN SPICE DRIZZLE
3/4 cup powdered sugar
1 tablespoon canned pumpkin puree
1 tablespoon heavy cream
1/8 teaspoon ground cinnamon Pinch of ground ginger, ground nutmeg, and ground cloves

Instructions

Preheat oven to 450°F. Whisk together flour, brown sugar, baking powder, salt, and spices in a large bowl. Add butter; use a pastry blender or 2 knives to cut butter into flour mixture until crumbly and mixture resembles small peas. Freeze 5 minutes.

Whisk together pumpkin puree and 2/3 cup of the heavy cream in a 1 cup glass measuring cup. Add pumpkin mixture to flour mixture, stirring just until dry ingredients are moistened.

Turn dough out onto wax paper; gently press or pat dough into a 7-inch round (mixture will be crumbly). Cut round into 8 wedges. Place wedges 2 inches apart on a baking sheet lined with parchment paper. Brush tops of wedges with remaining 2 tablespoons cream just until moistened.

Bake in preheated oven until golden, 13 to 15 minutes. Transfer scones to a wire rack, and cool 5 minutes.

Prepare the Vanilla Glaze: Whisk together powdered sugar, 3 tablespoons of cream, and vanilla until smooth. Add up to 1 tablespoon cream, 1 teaspoon at a time, if needed, to reach desired consistency.

Prepare the Pumpkin Spice Drizzle: Whisk together powdered sugar, pumpkin puree, cream, cinnamon, ginger, nutmeg, and cloves until smooth.

Spread a thin layer of Vanilla Glaze on each scone, and drizzle with Pumpkin Spice Drizzle. Serve warm or room temperature.

Starbucks Turmeric Latte

Active ingredients
2/3 cup unsweetened almond milk
1 1/2 teaspoons honey
3/4 teaspoon ground turmeric
1/8 teaspoon ground cinnamon, plus more for garnish
1/8 teaspoon ground ginger
1/8 teaspoon black pepper (optional)
2 tablespoons hot brewed espresso

Instructions
Stir together almond milk, honey, turmeric, cinnamon, ginger, and, if desired, pepper, in a 2-cup glass measuring cup. Microwave on HIGH 1 minute.Using a milk frother, whisk almond milk mixture until frothy. Place espresso in a glass, and top with almond milk mixture. Sprinkle with cinnamon, and serve immediately.

Panera Bread Summer Corn Chowder

Active ingredients
4 tablespoons unsalted butter
1/2 cup red bell pepper
1/2 cup diced green bell pepper
4 minced garlic cloves
1 medium white onion, chopped
1 medium jalapeño pepper, seeded and finely chopped
1/4 cup all-purpose flour
5 cups low-sodium vegetable stock
1 1/2 cups heavy cream
4 cups fresh sweet corn kernels
1 russet potato, diced
2 teaspoons salt
3/4 teaspoon smoked paprika
1/2 teaspoon cracked black pepper
1/4 teaspoon ground cayenne pepper
2 plum tomatoes, diced
1 tablespoon fresh lime juice
1 tablespoon white wine vinegar
3 tablespoons chopped fresh cilantro

Instructions
Melt butter in a large, heavy-bottomed pot over medium heat. Add red bell pepper, green bell pepper, garlic, onion, and jalapeño to pot; sauté for about 4 minutes. Add all-purpose flour and stir continuously for 1 minute or until a thick paste forms.

Stir in vegetable stock, heavy cream, corn kernels, Russet potato, salt, smoked paprika, black pepper, and cayenne pepper. Bring the mixture to a gentle simmer; cover and cook for 20 minutes or until potatoes have softened and mixture has thickened.

Stir in tomatoes, lime juice, white wine vinegar, and cilantro; simmer for 5 minutes. Serve immediately.

Panera Broccoli Cheddar Soup

Active ingredients
3 tablespoons unsalted butter
1 onion, chopped
2 garlic cloves, minced
1/4 cup all-purpose flour
3 cups chicken broth
1 cup whole milk
1 cup heavy cream
1/4 teaspoon white pepper
1/4 teaspoon black pepper
1/4 teaspoon ground nutmeg
1/4 teaspoon ground turmeric
4 cups broccoli florets (about 1 large head)
1/2 cup shredded carrots
8 ounces shredded sharp cheddar cheese (about 2 cups)

Instructions
Melt butter in a large saucepan over medium heat. Add onions and garlic to pan; sauté until fragrant and slightly translucent, but not brown, about 3-4 minutes. Stir in the flour to form a paste; cook 1 minute, stirring constantly.
Whisk in the chicken broth, milk, heavy cream, white pepper, black pepper, ground nutmeg, and turmeric powder. Simmer on low for 15 minutes or until the mixture has thickened slightly.
Stir in the broccoli florets, carrots, and cheese; cover pan. Simmer for 5-6 minutes, or until the broccoli is tender; add salt to taste. Serve Immediately .

Chick-Fil-A Sandwich

Active ingredients
3/4 cup dill pickle juice
2 tablespoons granuated sugar
4 (4-oz.) boneless, skinless chicken breasts
1/3 cup whole buttermilk
1/4 teaspoon cayenne pepper
1 large egg
1 1/4 cups (about 5 3/8 oz.) all-purpose flour
3 tablespoons cornstarch
2 tablespoons powdered sugar
2 tablespoons powdered milk
1 1/2 teaspoons kosher salt
1 teaspoon black pepper
1/2 teaspoon paprika
1/2 teaspoon baking powder
1/4 teaspoon baking soda
2 1/2 cups peanut oil
2 tablespoons unsalted butter
4 hamburger buns, split
8 dill pickle chips

Instructions
Stir together pickle juice and granulated sugar in a shallow dish until sugar dissolves. Add chicken breasts; cover and chill 40 minutes. Remove from brine, and pat dry.

Whisk together buttermilk, cayenne, and egg in a second shallow dish. Whisk together flour, cornstarch, powdered sugar, powdered milk, salt, pepper, paprika, baking powder, and baking soda in a third shallow dish.

Dredge brined chicken in flour mixture to coat, and shake off excess. Toss chicken in egg mixture to coat, and then back to flour mixture to dredge again. Press flour mixture to adhere to chicken, and place on a wire rack. Chill 15 minutes. Heat oil to 325°F in a medium saucepan over medium-high.

Carefully add chicken breasts to hot oil, 1 at a time, turning occasionally, until cooked through, 4 to 6 minutes. Let drain on a wire rack set in a baking sheet lined with paper towels.

Heat a large nonstick skillet over medium. Spread butter evenly on cut sides of buns. Place buns, buttered side down, in skillet; cook until toasted, about 30 seconds. Place 2 pickle chips on each bottom bun, and top with chicken and bun top. Wrap each sandwich in a piece of aluminum foil, and let stand 3 to 5 minutes before serving

Chick-Fil-A Honey Mustard

Active ingredients
1/2 cup yellow mustard
1/3 cup honey
2 tablespoons corn syrup
1/4 teaspoon dark molasses
1/4 teaspoon tamarind paste
1/4 teaspoon kosher salt

Instructions
Whisk together all ingredients in a medium bowl until well blended. Chill until ready to serve. Store in airtight container in refrigerator up to 2 weeks.

Chili's Baby Back Ribs

Active ingredients
1/2 cup dark brown sugar
2 teaspoons kosher salt
1 1/4 teaspoons smoked paprika
1/2 teaspoon black pepper
1/2 teaspoon onion powder
1/2 teaspoon garlic powder
1/4 teaspoon cayenne pepper
1 slab baby back pork ribs
1/2 cup cola soft drink
2/3 cup ketchup
2 tablespoons water
1 tablespoon plus 1 teaspoon molasses
1 tablespoon white vinegar
1 teaspoon yellow mustard
1/8 teaspoon liquid smoke

Instructions
Preheat oven to 275°F. Stir together brown sugar, salt, paprika, black pepper, onion powder, garlic powder, and cayenne in a small bowl. Rub 3 tablespoons of spice blend all over ribs, reserving remaining spice blend. Place ribs in a piece of heavy-duty aluminum foil; pour cola over ribs. Fold edges of foil together, and seal. Place ribs on rimmed baking sheet; bake in preheated oven 2 hours and 30 minutes.

Combine ketchup, water, molasses, vinegar, mustard, liquid smoke, and reserved spice blend in a small saucepan over medium-high. Bring to a boil, stirring constantly. Reduce heat to medium-low; cover and simmer 10 minutes. Remove from heat. Remove ribs from oven. Adjust oven to broil. Line a rimmed baking sheet with aluminum foil. Carefully unwrap cooked ribs, and transfer ribs, bone side up, to prepared baking sheet; discard foil package. Brush ribs with sauce, and broil 2 minutes. Flip ribs, and brush with more sauce. Broil until bubbly, about 2 minutes. Serve with remaining sauce

Doritos Locos Tacos

Active ingredients
For the "Cool Ranch" shells
1 tablespoon tomato powder
1 tablespoon buttermilk powder
1 teaspoon onion powder
3/4 teaspoon sugar
3/4 teaspoon garlic powder
1/2 teaspoon cheese powder
1/2 (1-oz.) package ranch dressing mix
6 crunchy taco shells
1 tablespoon canola oil For the "Nacho Cheese" shells
1 1/2 tablespoons cheese powder
1/2 tablespoon buttermilk powder
1 teaspoon dehydrated sweet bell pepper
3/4 teaspoon cheesy taco seasoning mix
3/4 teaspoon onion powder
3/4 teaspoon tomato powder
1/2 teaspoon sugar
1/2 teaspoon garlic powder
6 crunchy taco shells
1 tablespoon canola oil For the taco filling
2 tablespoons all-purpose flour
1 tablespoon chili powder
2 teaspoons onion powder
1 1/2 teaspoons paprika
1 1/2 teaspoons salt
1/2 teaspoon sugar

1/2 teaspoon garlic powder
1/4 teaspoon ground red pepper
1/4 teaspoon turmeric
1/4 cup beef stock
1 teaspoon canola oil
1 1/2 pounds 85% lean ground beef
1 tablespoons cheesy taco seasoning mix
1 cup sour cream
 1 1/4 cups shredded lettuce
1 cup diced tomato
1 cup shredded cheddar cheese

Instructions

To make the "Cool Ranch" shells, preheat oven to 325°.

Place tomato powder and next 6 ingredients (through ranch mix) in the bowl of a food processor; pulse until well combined. Transfer spice mixture to a medium bowl. Working 1 taco shell at a time, brush the exterior of the taco shells with canola oil using a pastry brush; sprinkle the exterior of each shell evenly with the tomato powder mixture, tapping against the side of the bowl to remove any excess. As you finish coating each shell, arrange in a single layer on a large rimmed baking sheet.

To make the "Nacho Cheese" shells, place cheese powder and next 7 ingredients (through garlic powder) in the bowl of a food processor; pulse until dehydrated bell pepper is ground and all ingredients are well combined. Working 1 taco shell at a time, brush the exterior of the taco shells with canola oil using a pastry brush; sprinkle the exterior of each shell evenly with the tomato powder mixture, tapping against the side of the bowl to remove any excess. As you finish coating each shell, arrange in a single layer on the same large rimmed baking sheet with the "Cool Ranch" shells.

Bake the "Cool Ranch" and "Nacho Cheese" shells at 325° for 1 to 2 minutes on each side, or until lightly toasted.

To make the taco filling, whisk together flour and next 8 ingredients in a medium bowl. Whisk in beef stock; set mixture aside.

Heat oil in a large skillet over medium heat. Add beef to pan; cook the beef, stirring and "chopping" with a wooden spoon to break it up, until the beef begins to brown, about 3 to 4 minutes. Increase heat and stir in beef stock mixture; cook 1 minute. Stir in cheesy taco seasoning; cook stirring often until beef is cooked through and liquid has thickened. Remove from heat.

To assemble tacos, spoon ¼ cup beef mixture into each of the 12 shells; top meat evenly with sour cream. Evenly layer lettuce, tomato, and cheese onto each taco

Olive Garden Breadsticks

Active ingredients
1 (25-oz.) pkg. Parkerhouse Roll Dough , thawed
6 tablespoons (3 oz.) unsalted butter, melted
1 1/2 teaspoons garlic salt

Instructions
Roll each dough piece into an 8-inch stick, and place on baking sheets lined with parchment paper. Brush sticks with about half of the melted butter; let rise in a warm place (80° to 85°F), free from drafts, for 30 minutes.
Preheat oven to 375°F. Bake breadsticks in preheated oven 10 minutes, rotating pan halfway through. The breadsticks should only be lightly golden. Brush with remaining melted butter, and sprinkle with garlic salt. Serve warm.

Chipotle's Cilantro Lime Rice recipe

Active ingredients
1 teaspoon vegetable oil
2/3 cup white basmati rice
1 tablespoon lime juice
1 cup water
1/2 teaspoon salt
2 teaspoons coarsely chopped fresh cilantro

Instructions
In a heavy 2-quart saucepan, heat the oil or butter over low heat. If using butter, stir it occasionally until melted. Add the rice and lime juice and stir for 1 minute. Add the water and salt. Raise the heat and bring to a boil. Cover, turn down the heat to low and simmer until the rice is tender and the water is absorbed about 25 minutes. Fluff the rice with a fork and stir in the cilantro.

Arby's Grilled Chicken and Pecan Salad

Active ingredients
2 1/2 cups chicken breast grilled
1 cup of diced red apple
1 cup chopped pecans
1 cup of grapes sliced in half
1/2 cup chopped celery
1/2 to 3/4 cup of mayonnaise
1 tablespoon of lemon juice (juice of one small lemon)
salt and pepper to taste

Instructions
In a medium-sized bowl add diced apple and one tablespoon of lemon juice. Stir lemon juice into apples coating them well. This will help keep the apples from turning brown. Add chicken, sliced grapes, diced celery, and pecans. Mix well until everything is mixed through. Add 1/2 cup mayonnaise, if the mixture is too dry you can add another 1/4 cup of mayonnaise. Add salt and pepper to taste. Allow flavors to marry in a covered bowl in the refrigerator for about 1 hour before serving.
o prepare sandwich like Arby's use thickly sliced wheat bread, add a couple of slices of green leaf lettuce, and add about 1 cup of chicken salad to the sandwich. While they do not toast their pecans, I think you could easily bring this salad to the next level by toasting the pecans in a skillet on medium-high heat just until they become fragrant. Allow the pecans to cool completely before preparing the chicken salad.

NUTRITION

Calories: 363kcal | Carbohydrates: 15g | Protein: 27g | Fat: 22g | Saturated Fat: 2g | Cholesterol: 72mg | Sodium: 143mg | Potassium: 669mg | Fiber: 3g | Sugar: 10g | Vitamin A: 150IU | Vitamin C: 6.2mg | Calcium: 34mg | Iron: 1.2mg

BJ's Pazookie Pizza Cookie

Active ingredients
1/2 cup Butter
1/2 cup Sugar
1/2 cup Brown Sugar
1 tsp Vanilla
1 Egg
1 1/2 cup Flour
1/2 tsp Baking Soda
1/4 tsp Salt
1/2 cup Chocolate Chips

Instructions
Preheat oven to 350.
Place small skillet or 8" round pan over low heat and melt butter.
Add sugar, brown sugar, beaten egg and vanilla. Mix well.
Add flour, baking soda and salt. Mix until well blended.
Add in chocolate chips and stir to evenly distribute.
Bake 15-20 minutes or until golden brown.
Allow to cool 10 minutes.
Cut into slices and top with vanilla ice cream.

Asian Zing Wings

Active ingredients
2 teaspoons cornstarch
4 teaspoons rice wine vinegar
1/2 cup corn syrup
1/3 cup sugar
1/4 cup Sriracha (or more)
1 tablespoon soy sauce
1 teaspoon lemon juice
1/4 teaspoon ground ginger
1/4 teaspoon salt
1/4 teaspoon garlic powder
1 egg yolk
3 teaspoons water
3 teaspoons cornstarch
1-2 dozen cooked wings

Instructions
Combine first 10 ingredients in a small sauce pan and stir to mix. Heat over medium heat. Reduce heat and simmer for 5 minutes, stirring occasionally.
Remove from heat and allow to cool. Combine egg yolk, water, and cornstarch in a small bowl and whisk until fully combined. Whisk mixture into cooled sauce.
Toss cooled wings in sauce and serve

Pan fried tilapia with bonefish grill's chimichurri sauce

Active ingredients
Pan Fried Tilapia
4 Tilapia Fillets
Bbq seasoning
salt and fresh ground black pepper
2 tsp olive oil
Bonefish Grill Chimichurri Sauce
Chimichurri Sauce
8 cloves garlic, minced
1 tsp. plus Kosher Salt
1 tsp. oregano, dry leaves
1 tsp. black pepper, ground
1 tsp. red pepper flakes
Finely grated lemon zest from 3 lemons
4 oz. fresh lemon juice
1 bunch flat leaf (Italian) parsley
1 cup olive oil

Instructions
PAN FRIED TILAPIA
Sprinkle each fish fillet on both sides with bbq seasoning, salt and fresh ground pepper.
Add 2 tsp olive oil into preheated pan over medium high heat. Place tilapia into pan and cook for about 3-4 minutes. Carefully flip fish over and continue to cook for another 3-4 minutes or until fish looks cooked through (will be white and flaky in middle).

Drizzle about 2 tablespoons of Chimichurri Sauce over each piece of fish. Serve with steamed veggies and enjoy!

CHIMICHURRI SAUCE

Combine all ingredients in a food processor and pulse chop until all ingredients are approximately 1/8 inch in size. Add Italian parsley and pulse chop until parsley is 1/8 inch in size. Add the olive oil and blend in quickly. (Do not over blend)

Allow the sauce to marinate for 30 minutes before serving.

Bang bang shrimp recipe

Active ingredients
1 lb shrimp 26-30, peeled & deveined
6 bamboo skewers optional
1/2 cup Bang Bang Sauce (click for recipe)
2 tablespoons chopped green onions sliced at an angle, divided

Instructions
If using skewers, place them in a shallow baking dish and cover them with water and soak them 10 minutes prior to using.
Pour half the sauce in a smaller bowl to use as a dipping sauce. Set aside.
If using skewers, thread 4-5 shrimp on each and brush the remaining sauce over the shrimp.
Heat a skillet or griddle over medium heat. Drizzle 2 tablespoons oil onto the skillet or griddle and place the shrimp in the skillet. Cook the shrimp 1-2 minutes per side, or until shrimp is opaque. (Adjust the cooking time if using different size shrimp.)
Transfer shrimp to a serving dish and brush lightly with the reserved sauce. Garnish with extra chopped green onions.
Serve immediately, with a dollop of dipping sauce, on the side. Enjoy!

Boston Market Sweet Potato Casserole

Active ingredients
Sweet Potato Layer
5 pounds sweet potatoes
4 tablespoons butter
2 eggs slightly beaten
1 teaspoon salt
1 teaspoon ground cinnamon
1/2 teaspoon vanilla extract
1/2 teaspoon ground nutmeg
1/2 cup dark brown sugar
1/4 cup heavy cream
Nonstick cooking spray
Cookie Crust Layer
1/2 cup all-purpose flour
1 cup dark brown sugar
1/4 teaspoon salt
1 cup quick-cooking oats
1/2 teaspoon ground cinnamon
1/4 pound butter
2 cups miniature marshmallows

Instructions

Preheat the oven to 350 degrees F.

Wrap sweet potatoes in foil, place them on a baking sheet and bake for about 1 hour. After 1 hour, test by piercing with a fork; if you can pierce them easily, they are done baking. If not, bake them a little longer and test again. Allow the sweet potatoes to cool until you can handle them, remove foil, and remove skins by simply pushing off the skins from the flesh of the potato.

Place the cooked potatoes into a large bowl. If using canned sweet potatoes, skip the baking. Just open the cans and drain off the syrup. Mash the sweet potatoes with the butter using a pastry blender or a potato masher until mostly smooth.

Add the eggs, salt, cinnamon, vanilla, and nutmeg and beat until you have a uniform mixture. Add the brown sugar and cream and mix well.

Oatmeal Cookie Crust

Combine the flour, brown sugar, salt, oats, and cinnamon in a medium bowl and stir together well. Stir in the 1/4 pound butter with a fork until you have a crumbly mixture. If you had turned off the oven, heat it again to 350 degrees F. Lightly coat a 9 x 13-inch baking pan with cooking spray.

Spreading the sweet potatoes in the pan. Top with the marshmallows, then crumble the oatmeal crust on top of the marshmallows. Bake 30 to 45 minutes.

Nutrition

Calories: 456kcal | Carbohydrates: 78g | Protein: 5g | Fat: 14g | Saturated Fat: 8g | Cholesterol: 64mg | Sodium: 483mg | Potassium: 704mg | Fiber: 6g | Sugar: 39g | Vitamin A: 27360IU | Vitamin C: 4.5mg | Calcium: 107mg | Iron: 2.9mg

Boston Market Creamed Spinach

Active ingredients
20 ounces spinach chopped, frozen, drained
1/2 cup Sour Cream
1 teaspoon Salt
2 tablespoon Butter
2 tablespoon chopped onion
1/4 cup Water
White Sauce
3 tablespoon Butter
4 tablespoon Flour
1/4 teaspoon Salt
1 cup Whole Milk

Instructions
Prepare the white sauce using a medium-low setting melt butter in a saucepan add flour and 1/4 teaspoon of salt until creamed together. Add milk a little at a time on medium heat. Constantly stir with a whisk until mixture becomes thick and smooth. Place butter in a 2-quart saucepan on medium heat, add onions.
Cook until the onions are transparent. Place spinach and add water to pan, lower the heat and place lid on pan. Stir several times until the spinach is almost completely cooked. Add 1 teaspoon of salt. When spinach is almost done add white sauce and sour cream, stir well and simmer until completely blended.
Recipe tips for the cook

Want to make this creamed spinach extra creamy? Add two or three tablespoons of cream cheese to the sauce!

You can use a couple of paper towels to help you squeeze out some of the excess water in the frozen spinach.

To make this extra savory, consider adding a tablespoon or two of blue cheese into the sauce!

NUTRITION

Calories: 186kcal | Carbohydrates: 10g | Protein: 5g | Fat: 14g | Saturated Fat: 9g | Cholesterol: 39mg | Sodium: 676mg | Potassium: 608mg | Fiber: 2g | Sugar: 3g | Vitamin A: 9340IU | Vitamin C: 27mg | Calcium: 162mg | Iron: 2.8mg

California Pizza Kitchen Original BBQ Pizza

Active ingredients
8 ounces chicken breasts grilled
1 tablespoon olive oil
2 tablespoons barbecue sauce (we use a spicy-sweet sauce).
For the pizza
16 ounces pizza dough
2 tablespoons semolina for handling the dough
1/2 cup barbecue sauce (we use a spicy-sweet sauce).
2 tablespoons Gouda cheese shredded
2 cups mozzarella cheese shredded
1/4 cup red onion sliced
2 tablespoons chopped fresh cilantro

Instructions
In a large frying pan, cook the chicken in olive oil over medium-high heat until just cooked, 5 to 6 minutes. Do not overcook. Set aside in the refrigerator until chilled through. Once chilled, coat the chicken with two tablespoons BBQ sauce; set aside in the refrigerator.

To make the pizza Place a pizza stone in the center of the oven and preheat to 500 degrees for one hour before cooking pizzas. Use a large spoon to spread 1/4 cup BBQ sauce evenly over the surface of the prepared dough within the rim. Sprinkle 1 tablespoon smoked Gouda cheese over the sauce. Cover with 3/4 cup shredded mozzarella. Distribute half the chicken pieces evenly over the cheese (approximately 18 pieces). Place approximately 18 to 20 pieces of red onion over the surface. Sprinkle an additional 1/4 cup mozzarella over the top of the pizza.

Transfer the pizza to the oven; bake until the crust is crisp and golden and the cheese at the center is bubbly (about 8 to 10 minutes). When the pizza is cooked, carefully remove it from the oven; sprinkle 1 tablespoon cilantro over the hot surface. Slice and serve. Repeat with the remaining ingredients for a second pizza. (The two pizzas may be prepared simultaneously if you are careful in placing the pizzas at opposite corners of your pizza stone.)

NUTRITION
Calories: 169kcal | Carbohydrates: 19g | Protein: 9g | Fat: 5g | Saturated Fat: 2g | Cholesterol: 22mg | Sodium: 438mg | Potassium: 98mg | Fiber: 0g | Sugar: 5g | Vitamin A: 135IU | Vitamin C: 0.4mg | Calcium: 88mg | Iron: 1mg

California Pizza Kitchen Chicken Tequila Fettuccine

Active ingredients

3 tablespoons unsalted butter (reserve tablespoon per saute)
1/2 cup chicken stock
2 tablespoons tequila
2 tablespoons freshly squeezed lime juice
3 tablespoons soy sauce
1 1/2 pounds chicken breast diced 3/4 inch
1/4 cup red onion thinly sliced
1/2 cup red bell pepper thinly sliced
1/2 cup yellow bell pepper thinly sliced
1/2 cup green bell pepper thinly sliced
1 1/2 cups heavy cream
Optional Garnish
1/2 cup corn tortilla strips

Instructions

Prepare rapidly boiling, salted water to cook pasta; cook until al dente, 8 to 10 minutes for dry pasta, approximately 3 minutes for fresh. Pasta may be cooked slightly ahead of time, rinsed and oiled and then "flashed" (reheated) in boiling water or cooked to coincide with the finishing of the sauce/topping.

Cook 1/3 cup cilantro, garlic and jalapeno in 2 tablespoons butter over medium heat for 4 to 5 minutes. Add stock, tequila and lime juice. Bring the mixture to a boil and cook until reduced to a paste-like consistency; set aside.

Pour soy sauce over diced chicken; set aside for 5 minutes. Meanwhile cook onion and peppers, stirring occasionally, with remaining butter over medium heat. When the vegetables have wilted (become limp), add the chicken and soy sauce; toss and add reserved tequila/lime paste and cream.

Bring the sauce to a boil; boil gently until chicken is cooked through and sauce is thick (about 3 minutes). When the sauce is done, toss with well-drained spinach fettuccine and reserved cilantro.

For an optional garnish, and a nice crunch add about 1/2 cup of crisp corn tortilla strips to the salad.

Recipe tips for the cook

If you like it spicy, you can keep the seeds and veins in while chopping up the jalapeno peppers. If not, just remove them for a milder flavor.

When cooking the pasta ahead of time, make sure it's al dente (undercooked). Rinse it and add some oil to it to keep from sticking. When you are ready to serve, you can reheat it in boiling water to coincide with the finishing of the sauce/topping. Serve family-style or transfer to serving dishes, evenly distributing chicken and vegetables.

The California Pizza Kitchen has a great cookbook The California Pizza Kitchen Cookbook.

NUTRITION

Calories: 1077kcal | Carbohydrates: 91g | Protein: 57g | Fat: 51g | Saturated Fat: 28g | Cholesterol: 349mg | Sodium: 1057mg | Potassium: 1204mg | Fiber: 5g | Sugar: 5g | Vitamin A: 2600IU | Vitamin C: 89.2mg | Calcium: 119mg | Iron: 3.5mg

Cheesecake Factory Red Velvet Cheesecake

Active ingredients
Cake Ingredients
15.25 ounces Duncan Hines Red Velvet Cake Mix
3/4 cup water
1/4 cup sour cream
1/2 cup mayonnaise
3 eggs
1 egg yolk
1/4 teaspoon kosher salt
1/4 teaspoon vanilla extract
Cheesecake Ingredients
24 ounes cream cheese softened
3/4 cup granulated sugar
1 1/2 teaspoons teaspoons vanilla paste or extract
1/4 teaspoon kosher salt
3 eggs, at room temperature large
1/4 cup heavy cream at room temperature
1 tablespoon flour or cornstarch
For Cream Cheese Frosting
12 ounces cream cheese softened
4 ounces unsalted butter softened
Heavy pinch kosher salt
1 teaspoon vanilla paste or extract
20 oz powdered sugar 5 cups
3-4 Tablespoons heavy cream
1 to 1 1/2 4 oz bars of real white chocolate (not candy coating)

Instructions

Cake Instructions

To Make the Cake Preheat oven to 350F. Spray 2 9" cake pans with pan spray. Line the bottoms with rounds of parchment and spray again. Set aside. In a large bowl, combine the cake mix, water, sour cream, mayonnaise, eggs, and yolk, salt, and vanilla. Using a hand mixer, mix on low speed for about 30 seconds. Scrape the bowl. Increase speed to medium and beat for 2 minutes. Divide the batter evenly between the two pans and bake in the center of the oven for 22-25 minutes, or until the tops spring back when lightly pressed, and the cakes are just starting to pull away from the sides of the pan. Allow to cool in pans for 15 minutes and then invert onto cooling racks. Invert again, so cakes cool right-side up. Note, the cakes will dome quite a bit. Once cool, use a large serrated knife to slice off the entire cake dome as evenly as you can. You should have two even discs of cake approximately 3/4" thick. Wrap well and refrigerate.

Cheesecake Instructions

For the Cheesecake Place racks in the upper and lower thirds of the oven. Put a rimmed baking sheet on each rack. Preheat the oven to 300F. Spray 2 9" cake pans with pan spray. Line the bottoms with rounds of parchment and spray again. Don't skip the parchment, because you'll be turning these out once chilled.

Set aside. Bring 2 quarts of water to a boil. Put the cream cheese in a large bowl. Using a hand mixer, beat on medium-low speed until smooth. Add sugar, vanilla, and salt, and continue to beat until well combined and smooth. Scrape the bowl as necessary. Add the eggs, one at a time, beating well after each addition and scraping the bowl as needed. Whisk the cream and flour together, so there are no lumps. Beat this mixture evenly into the rest. Pour half of the batter into each prepared pan and smooth the tops. Pull out the top rack, place one of the cheesecakes into the rimmed baking sheet and then pour in boiling water to come up to the level of the batter, about 3⁄4". Carefully slide the rack back in. Repeat with the other pan on the lower rack. Bake 20 minutes. Carefully rotate each pan and then continue to bake an additional 10 minutes.

Turn the heat off, open the oven door for a few seconds to let some heat escape, and then close the oven door. Allow cakes to remain in the cooling oven an additional 30 minutes. Crack oven door open and let sit for 30 more minutes. Remove to racks and run a thin spatula around the inside of each pan to make sure the cakes have released from the sides. Cool completely, and then chill in the refrigerator for at least 4 hours or overnight. When cooled, turn cheesecakes out onto parchment-lined lined racks. Place lined rack on top of the pan, invert both and give a firm rap on the counter. The cheesecake should release from the pan with no problem. If you do have issues, set the bottom of the pan in warm water for 15 seconds and try again. Freeze the cheesecakes and then wrap well. Leave in the freezer until ready to assemble.

Cream Cheese Frosting

For the Cream Cheese Frosting In a large bowl, use a hand mixer to beat the cream cheese and butter together until smooth. Add the salt and vanilla and continue to beat until smooth and creamy. Slowly beat in the powdered sugar, scraping the bowl as necessary. Beat in the cream, a bit at a time, until you have a nice spreading consistency.

To assemble

To Assemble and Decorate It is easiest to assemble the cake on the stand or platter you'll be serving it on, so make sure it is a good 12" in diameter and is nice and flat. Using a vegetable peeler, shave the sides of the bars of white chocolate to make curls. Catch them on a piece of parchment or a plate and refrigerate until needed. Place a tablespoon of frosting in the center of your platter and then press one of the cake rounds down into it, making sure to center the cake. Spread 3⁄4 cup of frosting evenly over the cake layer. Place one of the frozen cheesecake rounds onto the frosting and press down lightly. Frost with an additional 3⁄4 cup of frosting. Place the other cake round on top of the frosting and press down gently. Top with another 3⁄4 cup of frosting and then finish with the last frozen round of cheesecake. Scrape the rest of the frosting out onto the top of the cake. Spread it out into an even layer and then spread the excess that extends over the edge of the cake thinly around the sides. Use an offset spatula to make a simple zigzag design in the frosting on the top of the cake. Press the white chocolate curls liberally around the sides of the cake. Leave in the refrigerator for at least 4 hours before slicing and serving with a signature tall swirl of whipped cream.

NUTRITION

Calories: 714kcal | Carbohydrates: 89g | Protein: 7g | Fat: 38g | Saturated Fat: 16g | Cholesterol: 170mg | Sodium: 595mg | Potassium: 205mg | Fiber: 0g | Sugar: 75g | Vitamin A: 950IU | Calcium: 116mg | Iron: 2.2mg

Cheesecake Factory Chicken Piccata

Active ingredients
1 1/2 pounds chicken breast
1/2 teaspoon salt
1/2 teaspoon ground black pepper
1 tablespoon butter
1 tablespoon oil
8 ounces portobello mushrooms sliced
2 teaspoons butter
1/4 teaspoon salt
1/4 cup butter
1/4 cup dry white wine
1 tablespoon lemon juice
1 tablespoon capers
2 tablespoons heavy cream
2 teaspoons fresh chopped parsley
Serve with cooked angel hair pasta or other type of pasta

Instructions
Slice chicken breasts in half, they should be about 3/8 to 1/2 inch thick after cutting. Place the chicken breast between plastic wrap and pound thin with a meat pounder. Pound chicken carefully until it reaches about 1/4 inch thick. Season chicken breast with salt and pepper. Heat a skillet over medium heat and add 1 tablespoon of butter and 1 tablespoon of vegetable oil.

Cook chicken breast until brown on both sides, remove from the pan. Reduce the heat slightly and mushrooms, 1 tablespoon butter, and a sprinkle of salt. Saute the mushrooms until they just begin to brown. Remove the mushrooms from the pan. Add dry white wine to the pan, and scrape the browned bits off the pan with a wooden spoon. Add butter and lemon juice to the pan, and stir in capers and add heavy cream. Raise heat until the the mixture begins to bubble. Return mushrooms and chicken to the pan. Stir in fresh parsley and serve immediately. Serve with cooked angel hair pasta or other pasta of your choice.

Cheddars Santa Fe Spinach Dip

Active ingredients
10 ounces frozen spinach thawed and drained
1//2 cup finely diced white onion
8 ounces cream cheese
1/2 cup shredded white Cheddar cheese
1/2 cup shredded Monterey Jack cheese
1/2 cup shredded mozzarella cheese
2 teaspoons minced garlic
2 teaspoons finely minced jalapeno pepper
1/2 teaspoon seasoned salt
1/2 cup sour cream
1/2 cup salsa
4 ounces corn tortilla chips

Instructions
Preheat the oven to 350 degrees. In a medium bowl, combine the spinach, onions, cream cheese, Cheddar cheese, Monterey Jack cheese, mozzarella cheese, garlic, jalapeno pepper, and seasoned salt. Stir until well blended. Spread into a 1-quart casserole dish and bake for approximately 30 minutes or until the top is nice and bubbly. Serve with sour cream, salsa, and warmed tortilla chips.

NUTRITION
Calories: 381kcal | Carbohydrates: 18g | Protein: 12g | Fat: 29g | Saturated Fat: 15g | Cholesterol: 77mg | Sodium: 765mg | Potassium: 369mg | Fiber: 2g | Sugar: 3g | Vitamin A: 6520IU | Vitamin C: 5.4mg | Calcium: 346mg | Iron: 1.8mg

Chipotle Mexican Grill Guacamole

Active ingredients
6 small ripe avocado s (if you are using the large ones 3 will do)
1/2 cup minced red onion
1 minced jalapeno pepper
1 chopped garlic clove
1 tablespoon lemon juice
1 tablespoon lime juice
1/2 teaspoon kosher salt

Instructions
Cut the avocados in half, scoop out the "meat" into a large bowl, and gently break them into smaller pieces, but leave them very chunky. Add the red onion, jalapeno, garlic, and lime juice. Mix the ingredients together and salt to your desired taste.

NUTRITION
Calories: 246kcal | Carbohydrates: 14g | Protein: 3g | Fat: 22g | Saturated Fat: 3g | Cholesterol: 0mg | Sodium: 156mg | Potassium: 745mg | Fiber: 10g | Sugar: 1g | Vitamin A: 220IU | Vitamin C: 17.2mg | Calcium: 20mg | Iron: 0.8mg

Copycat Wendy's Chili

Active ingredients
2 tbsp. extra-virgin olive oil
1 medium onion, chopped
1 medium green bell pepper, chopped
2 stalks celery, chopped
1 tbsp. tomato paste
1 1/2 lb. ground beef
3 tbsp. chili powder
2 tsp. ground cumin
1 tsp. garlic powder
Kosher salt
Freshly ground black pepper
1 (28-oz.) can crushed tomatoes
1 (15-oz.) can kidney beans, with liquid
1 (15-oz.) can pinto beans, with liquid
Shredded cheddar, for serving
Green onions, sliced, for serving

Instructions
In a large pot over medium heat, heat oil. Add onion, pepper, and celery and cook until softened, 5 minutes. Add in tomato paste, stirring constantly until darker in color, about 2 minutes more. Add ground beef and cook, breaking up meat with a wooden spoon, until no longer pink, about 6 minutes more. Drain fat and return to heat.

Add chili powder, cumin, and garlic powder, and season generously with salt and pepper. Pour in crushed tomatoes, then fill can halfway with water, swirling to catch any remaining tomato, and add to pot. Add beans and their liquid and stir to combine. Bring chili to a boil then reduce heat to low and let simmer until flavors meld and liquid is slightly reduced, about 40 minutes. Taste and adjust seasonings as necessary.

Serve chili topped with cheddar and green onions.

Honey Walnut Shrimp

Active ingredients
1 c. water
1 c. granulated sugar
1 c. walnuts
1 lb. shrimp, peeled and deveined
Kosher salt
Freshly ground black pepper
2 large eggs, beaten
1 c. cornstarch
Vegetable oil for frying
1/4 c. mayonnaise
2 tbsp. honey
2 tbsp. heavy cream
Cooked white rice, for serving
Thinly sliced green onions, for garnish

Instructions
In a small saucepan over medium heat, combine water and sugar and bring to a boil. Add walnuts and let boil for 2 minutes. Using a slotted spoon, remove walnuts and let cool on a small baking sheet.
Pat shrimp dry with paper towels and season lightly with salt and pepper. Place eggs in a shallow bowl and cornstarch in another shallow bowl. Dip shrimp in eggs, then in cornstarch coating well.

In a large skillet over medium heat, heat 1" of oil. Add shrimp in batches and fry until golden, 3 to 4 minutes. Remove with a slotted spoon and place on a paper towel lined plate.

In a medium bowl, whisk together mayonnaise, honey, and heavy cream. Toss shrimp in sauce. Serve over rice with candied walnuts and garnish with green onions.

Asian Chicken Lettuce Wraps

Active ingredients
3 tbsp. hoisin sauce
2 tbsp. low-sodium soy sauce
2 tbsp. rice wine vinegar
1 tbsp. Sriracha (optional)
1 tsp. sesame oil
1 tbsp. extra-virgin olive oil
1 medium onion, diced
2 cloves garlic, minced
1 tbsp. freshly grated ginger
1 lb. ground chicken
1/2 c. water chestnuts, drained and sliced
2 green onions, thinly sliced
Kosher salt
Freshly ground black pepper
Large leafy lettuce (leaves separated), for serving
Cooked white rice, for serving (optional)

Instructions
Make the sauce: In a small bowl, whisk together hoisin sauce, soy sauce, rice wine vinegar, Sriracha, and sesame oil.

In a large skillet over medium-high heat, heat olive oil. Add onions and cook until soft, 5 minutes, then stir in garlic and ginger and cook until fragrant, 1 minute more. Add ground chicken and cook until opaque and mostly cooked through, breaking up meat with a wooden spoon.

Pour in sauce and cook 1 to 2 minutes more, until sauce reduces slightly and chicken is cooked through completely. Turn off heat and stir in chestnuts and green onions. Season with salt and pepper.

Spoon rice, if using, and a large scoop (about 1/4 cup) of chicken mixture into center of each lettuce leaf. Serve immediately.

Copycat McDonald's Shamrock Shake

Active ingredients
3 large scoops vanilla ice cream (about 1/4 c. each)
1/4 c. heavy cream
1/2 tsp. peppermint extract
6 drops green food coloring
Whipped cream, for topping
Maraschino cherry, for topping

Instructions
In a blender, mix vanilla ice cream, heavy cream, peppermint extract, and food coloring until completely smooth, then pour into a glass.
Top with whipped cream and a cherry before serving.

Crunchwrap Supreme

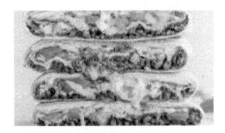

Active ingredients
1 lb. ground beef
1 tsp. chili powder
1/2 tsp. ground paprika
1/2 tsp. ground cumin
Kosher salt
Freshly ground black pepper
8 large flour tortillas
1/2 c. nacho cheese sauce
4 tostada shells
1 c. sour cream
2 c. shredded lettuce
1 c. chopped tomatoes
1 c. shredded cheddar
1 c. shredded Monterey Jack
1 tbsp. vegetable oil

Instructions
In a large nonstick skillet over medium heat, combine ground beef and spices and season with salt and pepper. Cook, breaking up meat with a wooden spoon, until no longer pink, about 6 minutes. Drain fat and wipe skillet clean.
Stack 4 large flour tortillas and place a tostada shell in the center. Using a paring knife, trace around edges of shell to cut 4 smaller flour tortilla rounds.

Build Crunchwraps: Add a scoop of ground beef to the center of remaining 4 large flour tortillas, leaving a generous border for folding. Drizzle cheese sauce over each, then place a tostada shell on top. Spread sour cream over each shell, then top with lettuce, tomato, and cheeses. Place smaller flour tortilla cutouts on top and tightly fold edges of large tortilla toward the center, creating pleats. Quickly invert Crunchwraps so pleats are on the bottom and they stay together.

In the same skillet over medium heat, heat oil. Add Crunchwrap seam-side down and cook until tortilla is golden, 3 minutes per side. Repeat with remaining Crunchwraps.

Copycat Chipotle Chicken

Active ingredients
FOR THE CHICKEN
1/2 red onion, roughly chopped
2 cloves garlic
1 chipotle pepper in adobo sauce, plus 2 tbsp. sauce
3 tbsp. vegetable oil
1 tsp. dried oregano
1/2 tsp. ground cumin
Kosher salt
Freshly ground black pepper
1 lb. boneless skinless chicken breasts
FOR THE BOWLS
Cooked Rice
Corn
Black beans
Guacamole
Salsa
Lime wedges

Instructions
In a food processor, blend onion, garlic, chipotle pepper and adobo sauce, oil, oregano, and cumin until smooth. Season with salt and pepper.
Add marinade and chicken to a large resealable plastic bag and rub all over to coat chicken. Let marinate in the fridge at least 2 hours.

Bring chicken to room temperature and preheat grill to high.
Grill until cooked through, 8 minutes per side.
Serve chicken over rice with desired toppings.

Mrs. Fields Chocolate Chip Cookies

Active ingredients
1 c. (2 sticks) butter, cold, cut into cubes
1 c. packed dark brown sugar
1/2 c. granulated sugar
2 large eggs
2 tsp. pure vanilla extract
2 1/2 c. all-purpose flour
1 tsp. baking soda
3/4 tsp. kosher salt
2 c. chocolate chips

Instructions
Preheat oven to 350° and line two large baking sheets with parchment paper. In a medium bowl, whisk together flour, baking soda, and salt.

In another large bowl, using a hand mixer, cream together butter and sugars until mixture resembles coarse sand. Add eggs and vanilla and beat until combined. Add dry ingredients and mix until just combined, then fold in chocolate chips.

Using a medium cookie scoop, form dough into balls and place on prepared pans. Bake until golden, 13 to 15 minutes.

Sticky Orange Chicken

Active ingredients
2 large eggs, beaten
1/2 c. plus 1 tbsp. cornstarch, divided
1/4 c. all-purpose flour
Kosher salt
Freshly ground black pepper
2 lb. boneless skinless chicken breasts, cut into 1" pieces
Canola oil
2 cloves garlic, minced
1/2 tsp. freshly minced ginger
1/2 tsp. crushed red pepper flakes
2/3 c. freshly squeezed orange juice
2 tbsp. low-sodium soy sauce
1 tbsp. apple cider vinegar
2 tbsp. sweet chili sauce
2 tbsp. hoisin sauce
1 tbsp. brown sugar
Juice of 1/2 lemon
2 green onions, thinly sliced
Cooked white rice, for serving
GET INGREDIENTS Powered by Chicory

Instructions
Set up dredging station: In one bowl, add eggs, and in a second bowl, mix together ½ cup cornstarch and flour and season with salt and pepper. Coat chicken pieces in egg, then toss in cornstarch mixture, tapping off any excess.

In a large, deep skillet over medium-high heat, heat ¼" oil. Fry chicken in batches until golden and crispy, 4 to 5 minutes. Drain on a paper towel-lined plate.

In a saucepan over medium heat, heat 1 tablespoon oil. Add garlic, ginger, and red pepper fakes and cook 2 minutes. Whisk in orange juice, soy sauce, apple cider vinegar, chili sauce, hoisin sauce, brown sugar, and lemon juice and bring to a simmer.

Meanwhile, in a small bowl, whisk together remaining tablespoon cornstarch with 2 tablespoons water. Slowly whisk into sauce to thicken and simmer until sauce is syrupy, about 5 minutes.

Toss chicken with sauce and green onions. Serve over rice.

Molten Chocolate Cakes

Active ingredients
8 tbsp. unsalted butter, room temperature (plus more for muffin tins)
Cocoa powder, for dusting
2 2/3 c. semisweet chocolate chips, melted
1/2 c. granulated sugar, plus more for muffin tins
6 large eggs
2/3 c. all-purpose flour
1 tsp. vanilla
2 tsp. espresso powder
1/2 tsp. salt
Confectioners' sugar, for dusting

Instructions
Preheat oven to 400 degrees F. Generously butter 12 cups of a standard muffin tin. Dust with cocoa powder, and tap out excess. Set aside.

In a large bowl, cream the butter and granulated sugar until fluffy with a hand mixer. Add eggs one at a time, beating well after each addition. Gradually beat in flour and salt until just combined. Stir in chocolate until evenly incorporated.

Divide batter evenly among prepared muffin cups. Bake for 8-9 minutes, just until tops of the cakes no longer jiggle. Remove from oven and let stand 5 minutes. Place a large baking sheet on top of the muffin tin. Hold both pans together and flip them to invert cakes onto to the baking sheet. Quickly transfer to serving plates, bottom sides up. Dust with confectioners' sugar. Serve immediately.

BBQ Chicken Pizza

Active ingredients
Cooking spray
1 lb. refrigerated pizza dough, divided into 2 pieces
2 c. cooked shredded chicken
3/4 c. barbecue sauce, divided
1 c. shredded mozzarella
1/4 medium red onion, thinly sliced
1/3 c. shredded gouda
Pinch crushed red pepper flakes (optional)
2 tbsp. freshly chopped cilantro

Instructions
Preheat oven to 500°. Line two large baking sheets with parchment paper and grease with cooking spray. In a medium bowl, stir together chicken and 1/4 cup barbecue sauce.
On a lightly floured surface, roll out pizza dough into a large circle, then slide onto prepared baking sheet. Top each pizza with 1/4 cup barbecue sauce, then half the chicken mixture, spreading in an even layer and leaving 1" around the edge bare. Next add an even layer of mozzarella and red onion, then top with gouda. Sprinkle with crushed red pepper flakes if using. Bake until cheese is melty and dough is cooked through, 20 to 25 minutes. Garnish with cilantro before serving.

Chinese Chicken Mandarin Salad

Active ingredients
FOR THE SALAD
3 c. shredded lettuce
2 c. shredded red cabbage
2 c. shredded chicken
1/2 c. jarred mandarin oranges, drained
1 instant ramen packet, crushed (flavor packet discarded)
1/2 c. shredded carrot
1/3 c. sliced green onions
1/4 c. sliced almonds
FOR THE DRESSING
3 tbsp. rice wine vinegar
2 tbsp. honey
1 tbsp. sesame oil
1 tbsp. hoisin sauce
2 tbsp. soy sauce
1 tsp. minced ginger
1 clove garlic, minced
1/4 c. vegetable oil

Instructions
Make salad: In a large bowl, toss together lettuce, red cabbage, chicken, mandarin oranges, crushed ramen noodles, carrots, green onions, and sliced almonds.
Make dressing: In a small bowl, whisk together vinegar, honey, sesame oil, hoisin sauce, soy sauce, ginger, and garlic. Slowly drizzle in vegetable oil, whisking constantly until emulsified.

Before serving, drizzle dressing over salad and toss to combine.

Chai Latte

Active ingredients
6 cardamom pods
2 cinnamon sticks
1 star anise
2 tsp. whole cloves
1 tsp. black peppercorns
1 (1") piece fresh ginger, thinly sliced
1/3 c. packed brown sugar
4 c. water
6 black tea bags
1 tsp. pure vanilla extract
4 c. whole milk
Ground cinnamon, for garnish
Ground cardamom, for garnish

Instructions
In a small pot over medium heat, bring spices, sugar, and water to a boil. Reduce heat and let simmer for 5 minutes.
Bring mixture back to a boil, then add tea bags and vanilla and remove from heat. Cover and let steep for 10 minutes. Remove tea bags then strain tea and discard spices.
In a medium pot over medium heat, bring milk to a simmer. Turn off heat and use an immersion blender to froth milk.

To each mug, pour 3/4 cup chai tea and ½ cup warm milk, adjusting amounts according to preference. Top off each mug with milk foam and a sprinkle of ground cinnamon and cardamom.

Strawberry Dressing

Active ingredients
FOR THE DRESSING
1/2 c. strawberries, hulled and halved
3 tbsp. apple cider vinegar
1 tbsp. honey
1/3 c. extra-virgin olive oil
1/4 tsp. poppy seeds
FOR THE SALAD
8 oz. baby spinach
1 c. strawberries, hulled and sliced
1/3 c. crumbled feta
1/3 c. sliced, toasted almonds

Instructions
Make dressing: To a food processor, add strawberries, vinegar, and honey and blend until smooth. Pour in olive oil and blend until emulsified. Add poppy seeds and blend 1 second more.
To a serving bowl, add spinach, sliced strawberries, feta, and toasted almonds. Toss with dressing and serve immediately.

Copycat Taco Bell Stackers

Active ingredients
1 tbsp. extra-virgin olive oil
1 onion, chopped
2 cloves garlic, minced
1 lb. ground beef
2 tsp. chili powder
1 tsp. paprika
1/2 tsp. ground cumin
Kosher salt
Freshly ground black pepper
4 large flour tortillas
1 1/2 c. nacho cheese sauce
2 c. shredded cheddar

Instructions
In a large skillet over medium heat, heat oil. Add onion and cook until soft, 5 minutes. Add garlic and cook until fragrant. Stir in ground beef, breaking up meat with a wooden spoon, and cook until no longer pink, about 6 minutes. Drain fat.
Stir in spices and season with salt and pepper.
Spread a thin layer of nacho sauce over one side of each tortilla, then top with ground beef and cheddar. Fold tortillas in half to make quesadillas.

Heat a large nonstick skillet over medium heat. Working one at a time, add quesadillas. Cook until golden (but not too crispy!), about 2 minutes. Flip and immediately fold the tortilla into thirds. Cook 2 minutes more per side. Repeat with remaining quesadillas.

Copycat Dole Pineapple Whip

Active ingredients
3 c. frozen pineapple chunks
2 bananas, peeled and sliced (frozen)
3/4 c. coconut milk
1/4 c. sweetened condensed milk
Pineapple slices, for garnish
Maraschino cherries, for garnish

Instructions
Pulse all ingredients in a blender until combined.
Pour into a ziplock bag and snip off a corner with scissors. Pipe into glasses and garnish with a piece of pineapple and a maraschino cherry.

Quesarito

Active ingredients
FOR THE BEEF
1 lb. ground beef
1 tsp. chili powder
1/2 tsp. ground cumin
1/2 tsp. smoked paprika
kosher salt
Freshly ground black pepper
FOR THE CILANTRO-LIME RICE
2 c. cooked white rice
1 tbsp. lime juice
2 tbsp. finely chopped cilantro
FOR QUESARITO ASSEMBLY
8 large flour tortillas
1 1/2 c. shredded Cheddar
1 c. Nacho Cheese Sauce
1/2 c. sour cream

Instructions
Cook beef: Heat a medium skillet over medium-high heat then add beef, chili powder, cumin and paprika. Season with salt and pepper and cook until beef is no longer pink, about 6 minutes. Drain fat.
Make cilantro-lime rice: In a medium bowl, toss together white rice, lime juice and cilantro using a fork. Set aside.

Make quesadillas: Heat a large nonstick pan over medium-high heat. When the pan is hot, add a tortilla and sprinkle cheddar cheese all over. Top with a second flour tortilla and cook until the cheese has melted, about 2 minutes per side. Repeat with remaining tortillas and cheddar to make 4 quesadillas.

Build quesaritos: Working on a cutting board or plate, top the center of one quesadilla with some rice, meat, nacho cheese sauce and sour cream. Roll up into a burrito. Repeat with remaining ingredients.

Reheat the nonstick pan over medium-high heat. When the pan is hot, add two quesaritos and cook until the outside quesadilla is golden and slightly crispy, 3 to 5 minutes per side. Serve immediately.

5-Cheese Ziti Al Forno

Active ingredients
1 lb. ziti
4 tbsp. butter
2 cloves garlic, minced
4 tbsp. all-purpose flour
2 c. half and half
Kosher salt
Freshly ground black pepper
1 c. freshly grated grated Parmesan, divided
3 c. marinara
2 c. shredded mozzarella, divided
1/2 c. shredded fontina
1/2 c. grated romano
1/2 c. ricotta
1/2 c. Panko breadcrumbs
Freshly chopped parsley, for garnish

Instructions
Preheat oven to 375°. Grease a 9"-x-13" baking dish with cooking spray. In a large pot of salted, boiling water, cook ziti until al dente. Drain and set aside.

Make alfredo: In a large, high-sided skillet over medium heat, melt butter. Add garlic and cook until fragrant, about 30 seconds. Whisk in flour and cook until the mixture is bubbling and golden, 1 minute more. Slowly pour in half-and-half, whisking constantly. Bring mixture to a simmer and stir in ½ cup Parmesan. Let simmer until the sauce thickens, 2 to 3 minutes, then season with salt and pepper.

Stir in marinara, 1 cup mozzarella, fontina, romano, and ricotta, then add pasta and toss until everything is well coated. Transfer to prepared baking dish.

In a small bowl, mix together remaining ½ cup Parmesan and Panko. Sprinkle evenly over top of dish. Bake until golden and bubbly, about 30 minutes.5. Garnish with parsley and serve.

Copycat Olive Garden Breadsticks

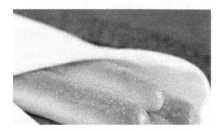

Active ingredients
1 1/2 c. warm water
1 (1/4 oz) package active dry yeast
4 c. flour, plus more for surface
2 tbsp. Butter, softened to room temperature
2 tbsp. sugar
1 tbsp. kosher salt, plus more for finishing
2 tbsp. butter, melted
1 tsp. garlic powder
Marinara, for dipping

Instructions
In a large bowl, combine water with yeast and set aside until foamy, 4-5 minutes. Next, add the flour, butter, sugar, and salt. Mix with a wooden spoon until all ingredients are fully incorporated and a dough has formed.

On a floured surface, knead the dough until smooth, about 3-5 minutes. Place on a large parchment sized baking sheet and cover with a kitchen cloth. Let rise for 45 minutes.

Meanwhile, preheat the oven to 400° F.

Cut into 12 small dough balls, knead, and stretch into breadsticks about 8 inches long and 1 inch wide. Place on a large parchment lined baking sheet and let rest for 10 minutes.

Brush with butter and bake until golden, 20 minutes.

Brush with more melted butter and sprinkle with salt and garlic powder. Serve.

Panera Autumn Squash Soup

Active ingredients

2 tbsp. extra-virgin olive oil
1 (2-lb.) butternut squash, peeled, and seeded, and cut into 1" cubes
2 medium carrots, peeled and chopped
2 large shallots, chopped
Kosher salt
Freshly ground black pepper
2 cloves garlic, minced
1 tbsp. packed brown sugar
2 tsp. ground ginger
1 tsp. curry powder
4 c. low-sodium vegetable broth
1 c. apple juice
1 c. water
1/2 c. pumpkin puree
2 tbsp. cream cheese, softened
Heavy cream (optional)
FOR THE TOPPING
1 tbsp. extra-virgin olive oil
1/2 c. pepitas
1/2 tsp. chili powder
Kosher salt

Instructions

FOR THE SOUP

In a large pot over medium heat, heat oil. Add squash, carrots, and shallots and season with salt and pepper. Cook, stirring occasionally, until beginning to soften, about 5 minutes. Stir in garlic, sugar, ginger, and curry powder, and cook until vegetables are beginning to caramelize, about 2 minutes more.

Pour over broth, apple juice, and water. Bring to a boil, then reduce to a simmer and cook until vegetables are soft, about 10 minutes.

Meanwhile, in a small bowl, whisk together pumpkin puree and cream cheese until incorporated.

Pour pumpkin mixture into pot and stir to combine.

Using an immersion blender, puree soup until smooth. Season with salt and pepper and stir in desired amount of heavy cream, if using. Serve soup topped with pepitas.

FOR THE TOPPING

Preheat oven to 350°. On a medium baking sheet, toss pepitas with oil and chili powder and season with salt.

Bake, shaking the pan halfway through, until pepitas are crunchy and golden, about 10 minutes.

Let cool completely.

Breakfast Crunchwrap Supreme

Active ingredients
FOR THE CRUNCHWRAP
4 frozen hash brown patties
5 large eggs
1 tbsp. whole milk
1 tbsp. butter
kosher salt
Freshly ground black pepper
2 tbsp. finely chopped chives
4 large flour tortillas
6 slices cooked bacon, chopped
1 c. shredded Cheddar
1 c. Shredded Monterey Jack
Vegetable oil, for pan
FOR THE CREAMY JALAPEÑO SAUCE
1/3 c. sour cream
Juice of 1/2 lime
1 jalapeño, minced
1/4 tsp. paprika
kosher salt
Freshly ground black pepper

Instructions
Bake frozen hash brown patties according to package instructions.

Make creamy jalapeño sauce: In a small bowl, whisk together sour cream, lime juice, jalapeño and paprika, then season with salt and pepper. Set aside.

Meanwhile, make scrambled eggs: In a large bowl, combine eggs and milk and whisk until frothy. In a medium nonstick pan, melt butter over medium heat. Pour egg mixture into the pan. Let set slightly then reduce heat to medium-low. Drag the eggs with a spatula or wooden spoon to create curds. When the eggs are almost cooked to your liking, season with salt and pepper. Fold in chives and remove from heat.

Assemble crunchwrap: Spread the jalapeño sauce onto the center of each flour tortilla, then top each with a hash brown patty, scrambled eggs, bacon, cheddar and Monterey Jack. Fold tortillas around the center, creating pleats. After wrapping, quickly invert crunchwraps so the pleats are on the bottom and they stay together.

Cook crunchwraps: In a medium nonstick pan over medium heat, heat a very thin layer of vegetable oil. Working one at a time, add crunchwrap seam-side down and cook until tortilla is golden on the bottom, 3 to 5 minutes. Flip crunchwrap and cook until the other side is golden, 3 to 5 minutes more.

Repeat with remaining crunchwraps. Cut each in half and serve warm.

BBQ Chicken Skillet Pizza

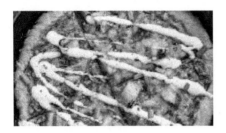

Active ingredients
1 tbsp. extra-virgin olive oil, plus more for brushing
1/2 lb. boneless skinless chicken breasts, cut into 1" pieces
Kosher salt
Freshly ground black pepper
All-purpose flour, for dough
1 lb. pizza dough, at room temperature
2 tbsp. barbecue sauce, plus more for drizzling
1/2 c. shredded cheddar
1/2 c. shredded fontina
1/4 small red onion, thinly sliced
Ranch dressing, for drizzling
Freshly chopped chives, for garnish

Instructions
Preheat oven to 500°. In a large skillet over medium-high heat, heat oil. Add chicken and cook until golden and no longer pink, 6 minutes per side. Season generously with salt and pepper.
Meanwhile, brush an ovenproof skillet with oil.
On a floured work surface, roll out dough until circumference matches your skillet. Transfer to skillet.
Leaving a 1/2" border for crust, spread barbecue sauce onto dough. Top with cheddar, fontina, chicken, and red onion.
Brush crust with olive oil and sprinkle with salt.
Bake until crust is crispy and cheese is melty, 23 to 25 minutes.
Drizzle with barbecue sauce and ranch and garnish with chives.

Frosted Lemonade

Active ingredients
1/2 c. freshly squeezed lemon juice
1/2 c. sugar
2 c. water
6 c. vanilla ice cream
sliced lemons, for garnish

Instructions
Mix lemon juice and sugar together in a pitcher until the sugar is fully dissolved. Add water to dilute and chill.
Into a blender, add lemonade and ice cream. Blend until smooth and divide among 3 cups. Garnish with slices of lemon and serve.

Bistro Box

Active ingredients
1/4 c. almonds
1/3 c. carrots
1 c. Grapes
1/4 c. pickle chips
1 tbsp. mustard
1 whole wheat tortilla
1 slice ham
1 slice cheddar
1/2 c. spinach

Instructions
Place almonds, carrots, grapes and pickle chips in your container.

Spread mustard onto your tortilla. Top with ham, cheese, and spinach. Roll into a pinwheel and slice into rounds. Place in container.

Nacho Fries BellGrande

Active ingredients
FOR FRIES
5 large russet potatoes, peeled and cut into thick strips
1 tbsp. olive oil
1 tsp. kosher salt
1 tsp. garlic powder
1 tsp. paprika
1/2 tsp. cayenne pepper
1/2 tsp. onion powder
FOR MEAT
1/2 lb. ground beef
1/2 tsp. chili powder
1/2 tsp. onion powder
Kosher salt
FOR CHEESE SAUCE
3 tbsp. butter
1 jalapeño, seeds removed and minced
3 tbsp. all-purpose flour
1 c. whole milk
2 c. shredded cheddar cheese
Kosher salt
FOR GARNISH
1 tbsp. sour cream
1/4 c. grape tomatoes, quartered
1 scallion, thinly sliced

Instructions

Make fries: Preheat oven to 400° and toss potato wedges in olive oil. Season with salt, garlic powder, paprika, cayenne, and onion powder and spread in an even layer on a large baking sheet. Roast 15 minutes, toss, and roast 15 minutes more, or until potatoes are tender in the center and crisped on the outside.

Make beef: In a medium skillet over medium heat, combine beef with chili powder and onion powder and season with salt. Cook until no pink remains. Drain fat and set aside.

Make cheese sauce: In a medium sauce pan over medium heat, melt butter. Add jalapeños and cook until fragrant, 2 minutes. Add flour and cook until slightly darkened, 2 minutes more. Add milk and bring to a simmer, then whisk in cheese and let thicken, 3 to 5 minutes more.

Assemble: In a shallow bowl, top fries with cheese sauce, beef, and garnish with sour cream, tomatoes, and scallions.

Smoked Mozzarella Fondue

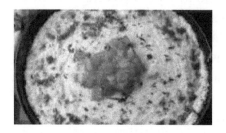

Active ingredients
8 oz. cream cheese, softened to room temperature
1 c. smoked mozzarella
1 c. provolone
1/2 c. freshly grated Parmesan
1/3 c. sour cream
1/2 tsp. dried thyme
1/2 tsp. Italian seasoning
1/4 tsp. red pepper flakes
kosher salt
Freshly ground black pepper
1 small tomato, chopped
1 tbsp. parsley, finely chopped

Instructions
Preheat oven to 350° F.
In a large bowl, combine cream cheese, cheeses, sour cream, thyme, Italian seasoning and red pepper flakes. Stir together until smooth and fully combined. Season with salt and pepper.
Transfer cheese mixture into a small skillet. Bake until cheese is bubbling, around 20-25 minutes. Broil if desired.
Garnish with tomato and parsley and serve with baguette.

Garlic Rosemary Chicken

Active ingredients

1 tsp. plus 2 tbsp. extra-virgin olive oil, divided
1 head garlic, top sliced off
4 chicken breasts, pounded 1/2" thick
kosher salt
Freshly ground black pepper
4 oz. cremini mushrooms, sliced
2 tbsp. unsalted butter, divided
1/4 c. white wine
3/4 c. chicken broth
3 sprigs fresh rosemary
5 oz. baby spinach
Juice of 1/2 a lemon
Mashed potatoes, for serving

Instructions

Preheat oven to 400°.

Drizzle a teaspoon of olive oil over garlic and wrap in foil. Bake until golden and soft, about an hour. Set aside to cool, then pick out cloves. Set aside.

In a large skillet over medium-high heat, heat remaining 2 tablespoons oil. Season chicken breasts with salt and pepper, then sear until golden, about 8 minutes per side. Transfer to a plate.

Return skillet to medium heat, add more oil if necessary, then add mushrooms. Season with salt and pepper and cook until slightly wilted, 5 minutes.

Add butter and let melt, then stir in the garlic cloves, white wine, chicken broth, and rosemary. Bring to a simmer, nestle back in chicken, and let simmer until sauce has reduced slightly, 6 to 7 minutes. Stir in spinach and lemon juice and let cook until spinach is slightly wilted, about 2 minutes more.
Serve with mashed potatoes.

Copycat Texas Roadhouse Rattlesnake Bites

Active ingredients
1 c. shredded mozzarella
1 c. Shredded Monterey Jack
2 jalapeños, minced
1 clove garlic, minced
1 c. all-purpose flour
kosher salt
Freshly ground black pepper
3 large eggs, beaten
1 c. plain bread crumbs
1 tsp. paprika
1/2 tsp. garlic powder
1/2 tsp. cayenne pepper
Canola or vegetable oil, for frying
Ranch dressing, for serving

Instructions
Line a large, rimmed baking sheet with parchment. In a large bowl, mix together cheeses, jalapeños, and garlic.

Using a tablespoon, scoop into balls and squeeze tight. Place on baking sheet and freeze until solid, at least 30 minutes.

Set up dredging station: In a shallow bowl, add flour and season with salt and pepper. In another shallow bowl, add eggs. In a third shallow bowl, add bread crumbs, paprika, garlic powder, and cayenne. Mix to combine.

Roll frozen cheese balls into flour, then eggs, and then bread crumbs, repeating until all are well coated.

In a large, deep skillet, heat 1/4" oil over medium heat until shimmering. In batches, fry bites until golden on all sides, about 3 minutes. Drain on paper towels.
Serve bites with ranch

Tonga Toast

Active ingredients
FOR THE STRAWBERRY COMPOTE
1 1/2 c. chopped strawberries
3 tbsp. sugar
1 tbsp. lemon juice
1 tsp. pure vanilla extract
FOR THE TOAST
1 loaf white bread, unsliced
2 Bananas, sliced
4 large eggs
1 c. heavy cream
1 tbsp. sugar
1 tsp. cinnamon
1 tsp. pure vanilla extract
Vegetable oil, for frying
1 c. cinnamon sugar
sliced strawberries, for serving
Maple syrup, for serving
GET INGREDIENTS Powered by Chicory

Instructions
Make strawberry compote: In a small skillet over medium heat, combine strawberries, sugar, lemon juice and vanilla. Bring mixture to a simmer and cook until the strawberries begin to break down and the mixture has thickened slightly, about 5 minutes. Remove from heat and gently mash the compote with the back of a fork (or a potato masher).
Slice bread into 3 to 4 very thick pieces. Use a knife to create a slit in one side of the toast, then stuff banana slices into the toast. Repeat with remaining bread pieces and bananas.

In a medium bowl, whisk together eggs, milk, sugar, cinnamon and vanilla. Dunk each stuffed sliced into the batter mixture, tossing to coat all sides.

Pour a 1/4" of vegetable oil into skillet and heat over medium heat. When the oil is hot, add the battered bread and cook until crispy and golden all over, about 2 minutes per side.

Drain toast briefly on a wire rack. Pour cinnamon sugar into a large shallow bowl, then gently shake off excess oil from warm toast and toss in cinnamon sugar.

Garnish with fresh strawberries and serve with strawberry compote and maple syrup.

Texas Cinnamon Butter

Active ingredients
2 sticks (1 cup) butter, softened
1/4 c. honey
1 tsp. ground cinnamon, plus more for sprinkling
1 tsp. kosher salt
1/2 tsp. pure vanilla extract

Instructions
In a large bowl, combine all ingredients. Using a hand mixer, beat all ingredients until fully combined and butter is slightly whipped.
Place butter in a ramekin and garnish with a sprinkle of cinnamon. Slather on everything.

Chicken Bake

Active ingredients
1/2 lb. bacon
2 tbsp. extra-virgin olive oil, divided
1 lb. chicken breast
1 tsp. Italian seasoning
kosher salt
Freshly ground black pepper
1/2 c. freshly grated Parmesan, plus more for sprinkling
1 lb. pizza dough
1/4 c. Caesar dressing
2 c. shredded mozzarella, plus more for sprinkling
2 green onions, thinly sliced
Egg wash
2 tbsp. chopped parsley

Instructions
Preheat oven to 425° and line a baking sheet with parchment paper.

In a large skillet over medium heat, cook bacon until crispy. Drain on a paper towel-lined plate then chop into small pieces. Wipe skillet clean.

To the same skillet, heat olive oil over medium-high heat. Season both sides of chicken breasts with Italian seasoning, salt and pepper. Add chicken to skillet and cook until golden on both sides, 6 to 8 minutes. Remove from skillet and let rest for 5 minutes before chopping into small pieces.

Divide pizza dough into two pieces. On a lightly floured surface, roll and stretch pizza dough to about 1/4" thickness.

Spread half the Caesar dressing onto pizza dough and top with half of each the chicken, bacon, mozzarella, Parmesan, and green onions.

Roll the pizza dough into a large log. Repeat with remaining ingredients.

Transfer logs to the prepared baking sheet. Brush with egg wash and sprinkle with more cheese and Italian seasoning.

Bake until golden and the dough is cooked through, about 25 minutes.

Garnish with parsley, then slice and serve warm.

Cilantro Lime Rice

Active ingredients
1 tbsp. butter
Juice of 2 limes, divided
1/2 tsp. kosher salt
1 c. basmati rice
2 c. water
1 tbsp. freshly chopped cilantro

Instructions
In a large saucepan over low heat, melt butter. Add juice from one lime, salt and rice, stirring for one minute to coat. Add water and bring to a boil.

Once boiling, cover and reduce to a simmer, cooking over low heat until rice is tender, 22 to 25 minutes.

Fold in cilantro, garnish with more lime juice and serve.

Crab Alfredo

Active ingredients
12 oz. fettuccine or linguine
3 tbsp. butter
3 cloves garlic, minced
3 tbsp. all-purpose flour
1 c. heavy cream
1 c. low-sodium chicken broth
1 1/2 c. freshly grated Parmesan, plus more for garnish
1 tbsp. Old Bay, plus more for sprinkling
kosher salt
Freshly ground black pepper
2 tbsp. freshly chopped parsley, plus more for garnish
1 lb. lump crab meat
Juice of 1/2 lemon

Instructions
In a large pot of salted boiling water, cook linguine according to package directions until al dente. Drain and return to pot.
In a large skillet over medium heat, melt butter. Add garlic and cook until fragrant, 1 minute, then add flour and stir until golden. Pour over heavy cream and chicken broth and simmer until thick, 3 minutes. Add Parmesan and let melt, 2 minutes.
Season with Old Bay, salt, and pepper. Stir in parsley and crab meat and toss until coated, then add linguine and toss until fully combined.
Garnish with Old Bay, parsley, and Parm and squeeze with lemon.

Creamy Chicken & Rice Soup

Active ingredients
3 tbsp. butter
1 onion, chopped
2 large carrots, sliced into rounds
2 stalks celery, thinly sliced
1 lb. boneless skinless chicken breasts
1 tbsp. fresh thyme leaves, plus more for garnish
3 cloves garlic, minced
kosher salt
Freshly ground black pepper
3 tbsp. all-purpose flour
4 c. low-sodium chicken broth
1 c. heavy cream
1 c. wild rice

Instructions
In a large pot or Dutch oven, melt butter. Add onion, carrots, and celery. Cook, stirring, until vegetables are tender and liquid has evaporated, 6 minutes. Add chicken and cook until golden, 10 minutes, then add thyme and garlic and stir until fragrant, 1 minute. Season generously with salt and pepper.
Add flour and whisk until golden, 1 minute. Pour over chicken broth and milk and season with salt and pepper. Add rice and bring to a simmer until rice is tender and chicken is cooked through.

McDonald's Cheddar Melt

Active ingredients
3 tbsp. butter
3 tbsp. all-purpose flour
1 1/2 c. milk
1 c. shredded Cheddar
kosher salt
Freshly ground black pepper
2 burger patties
1/2 small onion, finely chopped
2 tbsp. teriyaki sauce
2 rye buns

Instructions
In a saucepan over medium heat, melt butter. Add flour and whisk until totally combined. Cook until golden, 1 minute, then pour in milk and whisk until completely combined. Let thicken 3 minutes. Add cheddar and whisk until combined and creamy. Season with salt and pepper. Keep sauce on low heat while you prep the rest of the burger.

In a large skillet over medium-high heat, heat oil. Add burger patties and season with salt and pepper. Cook 4 minutes per side for medium rare. Set aside.

Add onions to burger fat in skillet and sauté until tender, 6 minutes, then add teriyaki sauce and stir until combined.

Assemble burger: On a rye bun bottom, place burger patty and top with cheese sauce and teriyaki onions.

Animal-Style Burgers

Active ingredients
4 tbsp. vegetable oil, divided
1 c. Onions, finely chopped
kosher salt
1/4 c. mayonnaise
1 tbsp. ketchup
1 tbsp. sweet pickle relish
1 tsp. white vinegar
1/2 tsp. sugar
4 thin ground beef patties, about 1/2-in thick
2 tsp. yellow mustard
4 slices American cheese
2 white hamburger buns
Lettuce, for serving
4 pickle chips
cooked frozen french fries, for serving (optional)

Instructions
Heat 2 tbsp. of vegetable oil in a large skillet over medium heat. Add the onions and cook until caramelized, about 20 minutes. If the onions are browning too quickly, turn down the heat and add a splash of water. Set aside onions and wipe the skillet clean.

Meanwhile, make the special sauce. Mix together mayonnaise, ketchup, relish, sugar and vinegar in a small bowl. Season to taste and set aside.

Heat the remaining vegetable oil in the pan over medium-high heat. Season both sides of the hamburger patties with salt and pepper before adding them to the pan. Cook for about 2-3 minutes, until the bottoms have developed a nice seared crust. Spread about 1/2 tsp of yellow mustard on the top (uncooked) side of each patty before flipping. Flip the patties and cook for another minute. Add the cheese slices on top of each patty and cook until the cheese melts.

Top each bottom bun with a heaping tablespoon of the sauce, a tomato slice, pickles and a piece of lettuce. Add a cooked patty to each bun and top each with caramelized onions. Top the onions with another patty each, then top with top bun. Serve with fries (garnished with extra sauce and onions).

Copycat Cheesecake Factory Shrimp Scampi

Active ingredients
1 lb. peeled, deveined shrimp, butterflied
1/2 tsp. baking soda
1 tsp. salt
1/2 package angel hair pasta
PARMESAN BREADING:
1/2 c. panko breadcrumbs
3 tbsp. shredded Parmesan, plus more for topping dish
1/4 tsp. Black pepper
1/4 tsp. cayenne pepper
CREAM SAUCE:
3 tbsp. olive oil
1 c. white wine
5 whole garlic cloves, peeled
1 pint heavy cream
1/2 red onion, diced
1 plum tomato, diced
1 tsp. fresh basil, chopped, plus more for topping

Instructions
Toss shrimp in baking soda and salt mixture. Leave in fridge for 15-20 minutes.
Cook angel hair pasta according to package instructions. Drain and set aside.
Make the Parmesan breading: Combine all ingredients in a shallow bowl. Coat shrimp in breading.

Warm olive oil in large skillet over medium heat. Use tongs to place the shrimp in the skillet. Cook shrimp, about 2 to 3 minutes per side, until it's curled up and is pink and white, not gray or translucent anymore. Place on a plate lined with paper towels.

Make the cream sauce: Add white wine and bring to a boil, stirring occasionally. Once boiling, reduce heat to medium-low and add garlic. Stir occasionally, letting the sauce reduce, for about 8 to10 minutes.

Add the heavy cream, stir and bring the sauce to a simmer. Add the onion, stir and let the sauce simmer for 5 to7 minutes. Add tomato and basil, stirring to combine. Season to taste with salt and pepper.

Divide angel hair pasta among plates. Top with shrimp and cream sauce. Garnish with additional Parmesan and basil if you'd like.

Skinny Burrito Bowl

Active ingredients
1 c. brown jasmine rice
1 lb. ground turkey
1 tbsp. Taco Seasoning
kosher salt
1/4 c. plain yogurt
2 tsp. Hot sauce
2 c. grape tomatoes, halved
2 avocados, diced
1 15-oz. can black beans

Instructions
In a small pot, cook rice according to package directions.
Meanwhile, in a large skillet over medium heat, cook turkey until no longer pink, 6 to 7 minutes. Season with taco seasoning and salt.
In a small bowl, mix together yogurt and hot sauce. (If you want a nice drizzle, transfer to a plastic Ziploc or piping bag.)
Assemble burrito bowl: Divide rice among four bowls and top with ground turkey, tomatoes, avocados, and black beans and drizzle with spicy yogurt. Garnish with cilantro.

Copycat DoubleTree Chocolate Chip Cookies

Active ingredients
1 c. (2 sticks) butter, softened
1 c. packed brown sugar
1/2 c. granulated sugar
1 1/2 tsp. pure vanilla extract
2 large eggs, room temperature
2 1/2 c. all-purpose flour
1 1/2 tsp. baking soda
1 tsp. kosher salt
1/4 tsp. ground cinnamon
1/3 c. quick-cooking oats
2 1/2 c. semisweet chocolate chips
3/4 c. chopped walnuts

Instructions
Preheat oven to 350°. Line two baking sheets with parchment. In a large mixing bowl using a hand mixer, cream butter, sugars, and vanilla until light and fluffy, about 5 minutes. Slowly mix in eggs, beating until mixture is smooth.

In a separate bowl, combine flour, baking soda, salt, and cinnamon. Gradually stir dries into the butter-sugar mixture, then fold in oats, chocolate chips, and walnuts.

Use a large cookie scoop to place balls of dough about 2" apart on prepared baking sheets. Bake until edges are lightly golden but center of cookie is still a bit soft, 17 to 19 minutes.

Avocado Egg Rolls

Active ingredients
3 avocados, diced
1/4 c. Chopped red onion
3 tbsp. chopped sun-dried tomatoes
2 cloves garlic, minced
1/4 c. chopped fresh cilantro
Juice of 1 lime
kosher salt
12 egg roll wrappers
Vegetable oil, for frying
1/3 c. sour cream
Few splashes hot sauce

Instructions
In a large bowl, stir avocados, red onion, sun-dried tomatoes, garlic, half the cilantro, and juice of 1/2 lime and season with salt.

Lay an egg roll wrapper on a clean surface in a diamond shape and spoon two tablespoons (max) of the mixture in the center. Fold up the bottom half and tightly fold in the sides. Gently roll, then seal the fold with a couple drops of water. Repeat until filling is all used up.

In a large skillet, add enough oil to reach 1" up the side of the pan. Heat until it starts to bubble. Add egg rolls and fry until golden, 1 minute per side. Transfer to a paper towel-lined plate.

Make dipping sauce: In a small bowl stir together sour cream, remaining lime juice, remaining cilantro, and hot sauce.

Serve egg rolls with dipping sauce.

Mongolian Beef

Active ingredients
1/4 c. plus 1 tbsp. vegetable oil, divided
2 cloves garlic, minced
1 tbsp. minced fresh ginger
3/4 c. soy sauce
1/2 c. water
1/2 c. brown sugar
1 lb. flank steak, sliced against the grain
1/4 c. cornstarch
4 green onions, sliced into quarters, plus 1 chopped green onion for garnish
Butter lettuce, for serving

Instructions
In a small saucepan over medium heat, heat 1 tablespoon vegetable oil. Add garlic and ginger and cook until fragrant, 2 minutes. Add soy sauce, water and brown sugar and stir until dissolved. Bring to a boil, then reduce heat and simmer until reduced by half, 10 to 12 minutes.

Meanwhile, in a large skillet over medium heat, heat remaining 1/4 cup vegetable oil.

In a large bowl, toss flank steak with cornstarch until fully coated. Add steak to skillet and sear until crispy, 3 to 4 minutes per side. Drain fat.

Add sauce and green onion quarters to skillet and toss until combined, then simmer a few minutes more.

Serve steak in lettuce cups and garnish with green onions.

Make-Ahead Bacon & Egg Sandwiches

Active ingredients
Cooking spray
12 large eggs
kosher salt
Freshly ground black pepper
12 slices bacon
Butter, for English muffins
12 English muffins
12 slices cheddar

Instructions
Preheat oven to 350°.

Spray muffin tin with nonstick baking spray. Crack eggs into the tin, season with salt and pepper and bake until egg whites are set, 15 minutes.

Meanwhile, cook bacon until crispy. Drain and set aside.

Spread butter on English Muffins and toast in oven until golden brown, about 5 minutes.

Assemble sandwiches with egg, cheese and bacon.

Heat in oven to eat right away, or wrap in foil. If wrapping, write date and then freeze. Reheat in oven at 350° until warmed through.

Copycat Chili's Cajun Chicken Pasta

Active ingredients
1/2 box penne
2 boneless skinless chicken breasts (thin cut)
1 tbsp. Cajun seasoning
3 tbsp. butter, divided
1 pt. half-and-half
1/2 tsp. garlic powder
kosher salt
Freshly ground black pepper
1/3 c. plus 3 tbsp. freshly grated Parmesan
1 diced tomato
1 tsp. sliced flat-leaf parsley

Instructions
Cook penne according to package instructions. Drain and set aside.

Pat chicken dry with a paper towel and dust both sides with Cajun seasoning until thoroughly coated. In a large sauté pan over medium heat, melt 1 tablespoon butter. Add chicken, cooking through completely, about 5 to 6 minutes for each side. Remove chicken from skillet and set aside.

Add remaining 2 tablespoons butter to skillet, along with half-and-half, garlic powder, salt and pepper and 1/3 cup Parmesan. Stir until combined and remove from heat.

Toss pasta in sauce and divide onto two plates (there will be some leftover). Slice chicken and place atop pasta. Sprinkle each with remaining Parmesan, diced tomatoes and parsley and serve.

Copycat Starbucks Chocolate Chunk Cookies

Active ingredients
2 sticks butter
3/4 c. dark brown sugar
3/4 c. granulated sugar
1 large egg
1 1/2 tsp. pure vanilla extract
2 c. wheat flour
1 tsp. baking soda
1/2 tsp. kosher salt
1 1/2 c. semisweet chocolate chunks (plus more for topping cookies)

Instructions
Preheat oven to 375°. As it heats, cream the butter and both types of sugar together until light and fluffy, 2 to 3 minutes. Add egg and vanilla, beating to combine.

In a separate bowl, combine flour, baking soda, and salt. Slowly mix in flour mixture, then fold in chocolate chunks.

Roll into 1 1/2" balls, placing them about 2 inches apart on a parchment-lined baking sheet. Top each cookie with a few extra chocolate chunks, for presentation's sake, and bake for 8 to 10 minutes, or until the cookie is lightly golden and no longer gooey in the center.

Copycat Olive Garden Zuppa Toscana

Active ingredients
1 lb. Hot Italian sausage, casings removed
1 large onion, chopped
3 cloves garlic, minced
kosher salt
Freshly ground black pepper
6 c. low-sodium chicken broth
4 large russet potatoes, diced
1 bunch curly kale, leaves stripped and chopped
3/4 c. heavy cream
4 slices cooked bacon, chopped
1/4 freshly grated Parmesan, for serving

Instructions
In a large pot over medium heat, cook sausage, breaking up with the back of a wooden spoon, until browned and no longer pink, 5 to 7 minutes. Transfer to a plate to drain.

Add onion to pot and let cook until soft, 5 minutes, then add garlic and cook until fragrant, 1 minute more. Season with salt and pepper. Add chicken broth and potatoes and cook until potatoes are tender, 23 to 25 minutes.

Stir in kale and let cook until leaves are tender and bright green, 3 minutes, then stir in heavy cream, sausage, and bacon and simmer 5 minutes more.

Season with pepper, garnish with Parm, and serve.

Copycat Red Lobster Cheddar Bay Biscuits

Active ingredients
3 c. all-purpose flour
2 tbsp. baking powder
1/4 tsp. kosher salt
1 1/2 sticks butter, cold and chopped
1 3/4 c. whole milk
2 tsp. garlic powder
1 1/2 c. shredded sharp Cheddar
1/2 c. butter
1 tbsp. Freshly Chopped Parsley
1 tsp. garlic powder

Instructions
Preheat oven to 400°. Combine flour, baking powder, salt and butter in a large mixing bowl and use an electric mixer to combine, starting slow and working your way up to medium speed, until you've formed a dough with pea-sized lumps. Slowly add in milk (keep the mixer on low to avoid splashes).
Fold in garlic powder and cheese. Use a spoon to place 2" blobs of dough onto a parchment-lined baking sheet. Bake until lightly golden, 18 to 20 minutes.
Melt butter in 20-second intervals in the microwave, stirring in between, until fully melted. Stir in parsley and garlic powder. Brush mixture on top of each biscuit as soon as they're out of the oven and serve immediately.

Copycat Olive Garden Salad Dressing

Active ingredients
1/2 c. extra-virgin olive oil
1/4 c. mayonnaise
Juice of 1 lemon
1 packet Italian seasoning
1 clove garlic, minced
1 tbsp. freshly grated Pecorino Romano or Parmesan
kosher salt

Instructions
In a small bowl, whisk together ingredients and season with salt.

Copycat Chick-fil-A Chicken Sandwich

Active ingredients
1 large egg
1/2 c. milk
1 tsp. paprika
2 tbsp. water
1 c. all-purpose flour
1/2 c. whole-wheat flour
1 tbsp. powdered milk
1 tbsp. confectioners' sugar
1/4 tsp. baking soda
1/4 tsp. dry mustard
kosher salt
Freshly ground black pepper
2 c. peanut oil, for frying
2 boneless skinless chicken breasts
Pickles, for serving
Butter, for bread
2 Hamburger buns

Instructions
In shallow baking dish, whisk egg, milk, ½ teaspoon paprika, and water together. In another baking dish, whisk both flours, powdered milk, confectioners' sugar, baking soda, dry mustard, and remaining ½ teaspoon paprika and season with salt and pepper.Meanwhile, heat about two inches of peanut oil to 325 degrees F in a heavy-bottomed pot or cast iron skillet. While oil heats, slice pickle, and set aside.

Working in batches, dip chicken in the egg mixture, turning to coat, then dredge in flour mixture and shake off any excess. Fry the chicken in hot oil, using a candy thermometer to monitor oil temperature, until golden brown, about 4 minutes. Drain on paper towels.

Heat a large skillet over medium heat. Spread the cut side of the buns with some butter, and lightly toast in the skillet, buttered-side down. To assemble sandwiches, spread grilled buns with more butter, dip 2 pickle slices in jarred pickle juice to moisten and place on the bottom bun. Top with a piece of fried chicken and the bun top.

Copycat Chipotle Carnitas

Active ingredients
3 lb. boneless pork shoulder
kosher salt
Freshly ground black pepper
2 cloves garlic, minced
1 1/2 c. low-sodium chicken broth
3 bay leaves
4 sprigs fresh thyme (or 1 tsp. dried)
Juice of 1 lemon
2 sprigs rosemary (or 1/2 tsp. dried)

Instructions
Use a fork to poke holes in the pork shoulder, then sprinkle both sides with salt and pepper and rub on minced garlic. Place pork in the slow cooker.
Add chicken broth, bay leaves, thyme, lemon juice and rosemary. Cover and cook for 6 to 8 hours.
Remove pork from slow cooker and place in a separate bowl. Use two forks to shred meat, then serve.

Copycat Panera Chocolate Chip Cookies

Active ingredients
2 1/2 sticks unsalted butter
1 1/4 c. dark brown sugar
1/4 c. granulated sugar
2 tsp. vanilla extract
2 eggs
3 1/2 c. all-purpose flour
1 tbsp. cornstarch
1 tsp. baking soda
1 tsp. salt
1 bag mini semisweet chocolate chips (12 ounces)

Instructions
Using an electric mixer, beat butter and sugars together until light and fluffy. Slowly add in vanilla extract and eggs, whipping until combined.

In a separate bowl, mix the flour, cornstarch, baking soda and salt. Stir it into the butter mixture. Fold in mini chocolate chips. Roll dough into 1 1/2-inch balls, flattening them slightly, and placing them about 2 inches apart on a parchment-lined baking sheet. Freeze for 15 minutes, so they're more likely to hold their shape.

When you place them in the freezer, preheat the oven to 350°F. Bake the cookies for 13-15 minutes, or until lightly golden on the edges.

Cracker Barrel-Inspired Broccoli Cheddar Chicken Casserole

Active ingredients
4 boneless skinless chicken breasts
Kosher salt
Freshly ground black pepper
1 c. whole milk
1 (10.5-oz.) can cheddar cheese soup
1/2 tsp. paprika
1 c. shredded sharp cheddar
1 (10-oz.) bag frozen broccoli florets
1 c. crushed Ritz crackers, divided

Instructions
Preheat oven to 350°. Pat each chicken breast dry using paper towels. Season with salt and pepper and place in a large oven-proof casserole dish.

In a large mixing bowl, combine milk, soup, paprika, and cheddar, then fold in broccoli and half the crackers. Pour over chicken, covering entirely.

Top with remaining crackers and bake until chicken is fully cooked, 45 minutes.

Copycat Tate's Chocolate Chip Cookies

Active ingredients
2 c. all-purpose flour
1/2 tsp. baking soda
1/2 tsp. salt
2 sticks salted butter, room temperature
3/4 c. sugar
3/4 c. brown sugar
1 1/2 tsp. vanilla extract
2 Eggs, room temperature
1 bag semisweet chocolate chips (about 12 ounces)
coarse sea salt (for topping cookies)

Instructions
Preheat the oven to 350°F. As it heats, combine the flour, baking soda and salt in a large mixing bowl. Set aside.

In a large mixing bowl, combine sugars and butter. Use an electric mixer to beat the two together, whipping them until the mixture is a pale yellow and has a creamy texture. Slowly beat in the eggs and vanilla extract.

Stir in the flour mixture, adding a little at a time until fully combined. Fold in the chocolate chips.

Form into 1-inch patties and place about 1-2 inches apart on a parchment-lined baking sheet. Sprinkle each with a little coarse sea salt.

Bake for 15-17 minutes, or until the cookies are a warm, golden brown and look crispy on the edges.

Copycat Levain Bakery Cookies

Active ingredients
2 c. all-purpose flour
1 1/4 c. cake flour
2 tsp. baking powder
1/4 tsp. baking soda
1/4 tsp. kosher salt
1 c. (2 sticks) cold butter, cubed
2/3 c. packed brown sugar
2/3 c. granulated sugar
2 c. dark chocolate chips
1 c. very coarsely chopped walnuts, lightly toasted
2 large eggs, lightly beaten

Instructions
Line two large baking sheets with parchment paper. In a medium bowl, whisk together flours, baking powder, baking soda, and kosher salt.

In a large bowl using a hand mixer (or in the bowl of a stand mixer), cream cold butter on low speed until cubes lose half their shape, about 30 to 45 seconds. Add sugars and continue to cream briefly, 30 to 60 seconds more. Add chocolate and walnuts and beat until combined.

Gradually add flour mixture and beat to combine; mixture will be a bit crumbly. If any big pieces of butter remain, use hands to cut butter into smaller pieces. Add in eggs and beat until fully combined and smooth, forming a cohesive dough.

Portion large balls of dough, about 6 ounces or ¾ cup each. Place 4 balls of dough on each prepared tray and place in freezer. Let chill for 90 minutes.

When ready to bake, preheat oven to 375°. Place one empty baking sheet upside-down in oven and place one tray of frozen dough on top. Bake one sheet of cookies at a time, until edges and spots on top are golden, but insides are still slightly doughy, about 26 minutes.

Chewy Chocolate-Coconut Cookies

Active ingredients
1 c. unsalted butter
1/2 c. granulated sugar
1/2 tsp. vanilla extract
2 c. all-purpose flour
1/4 tsp. baking powder
1/4 tsp. salt
Caramel-Coconut Sauce (see recipe below)
2 c. semisweet chocolate chips
3 tsp. vegetable, canola, or other flavorless oil
CARAMEL-COCONUT SAUCE
2 c. sweetened coconut flakes
1 1/2 c. granulated sugar
1/2 c. heavy cream
4 tbsp. unsalted butter

Instructions
In the bowl of a stand mixer fitted with the paddle attachment, cream together butter and sugar on medium-high speed until light and fluffy, 3 to 4 minutes. Add vanilla extract and mix to incorporate.

In a medium mixing bowl, whisk together flour, baking powder, and salt. With the mixer speed on low, add the dry ingredients and mix until just combined. Turn the dough out onto a work surface and form into a disc. Wrap in plastic wrap and refrigerate for at least one hour.

Preheat oven to 325 degrees F. Line baking sheets with parchment paper or a silicone baking mat.

Roll cookie dough to 1/4-inch thickness on a lightly floured surface and cut dough into 2-inch circles. Cut a small circle in the center with another circular cutter or a straw to create a "ring" shape. Transfer cookie dough to prepared baking sheets.

Bake cookies for 15 to 18 minutes, until lightly browned at the edges. Cool on the baking sheets for 10 minutes, then transfer to a wire rack to cool completely.

To make the Coconut-Caramel Sauce: Place coconut flakes in a skillet over medium heat. Stir constantly, until coconut is lightly browned. Remove from heat.

Heat sugar to a medium saucepan over medium-high heat, stirring often so the sugar does not burn. The sugar will form clumps, then melt into a liquid and start to brown. Once all the sugar has dissolved and the liquid is dark amber in color, remove it from the heat. Pour in the cream and whisk constantly until the mixture stops bubbling and becomes smooth again. Whisk in the butter until melted and combined.

Use a small offset spatula or the back of a spoon to spread a thin layer of warm caramel over each cookie. Pour 1 cup of the remaining caramel over the toasted coconut and stir to coat. You want the coconut to be just lightly coated with caramel, not swimming in it. Use your offset spatula or spoon to spread the coconut mixture over the caramel layer of each cookie and use a toothpick to clear it away from the center hole. Allow the caramel to set up (chilling the cookies speeds this up.)

Line a baking sheet with parchment or wax paper. Heat chocolate chips in the microwave, stirring every 15 seconds, until melted and smooth. Stir in oil to thin out the chocolate. Carefully dip the bottoms of each cookie in the chocolate mixture and place on the prepared baking sheet. Dip a fork in the chocolate and drizzle lines of chocolate over the top of each cookie (you may need to warm up the chocolate again if it has cooled slightly and become too thick to drizzle). Let chocolate set up at room temperature or in the refrigerator before serving.

Sprinkles Red Velvet Cupcakes with Cream Cheese Frosting

Active ingredients
1 1/3 cups all-purpose flour
3 Tbsp cocoa powder
1/2 tsp baking soda
3/4 cup salted butter , firm but not cold*
1 cup + 2 Tbsp granulated sugar
2 large eggs
1 Tbsp red food coloring
2 tsp vanilla extract
1/2 cup whole milk
1 tsp distilled white vinegar

1 recipe Cream Cheese Frosting
Cream Cheese Frosting
1/2 cup salted butter , firm but not cold (if using unsalted add 1/8 tsp salt)
6 oz cream cheese , cold (I recommend using Philadelphia brand in this recipe)
1/2 tsp vanilla extract
3 1/2 cups powdered sugar
Red and blue food coloring , for decor (optional)

Instructions

Preheat oven to 350 degrees. In a mixing bowl, whisk together flour, cocoa powder and baking soda, set aside. In a separate large mixing bowl, with an electric hand mixer on medium speed, whip together butter and sugar until pale and fluffy, about 3-4 minutes. Add in eggs one at a time stirring after each addition. (Now stand back and change out of any nice shirt you have on and) Add red food coloring and vanilla extract and mix until combine. In a small mixing bowl (or in the measuring cup you used to measure milk), combine milk and 1 tsp vinegar. Add milk mixture and flour mixture to cupcake mixture, alternating in two separate batches, mixing until combine after each addition. Divide batter evenly among 15 paper lined muffin cups, filling each cup about 2/3 full. Bake in preheated oven 18-21 minutes until toothpick inserted into center of cupcake comes out clean. Remove from oven and allow to cool about 2 minutes in muffin tin, then transfer to wire rack to cool for 10 minutes, then transfer to an airtight container to cool completely (this just helps them retain more moisture). Once cooled completely, spread generously with Cream Cheese Frosting (just as sprinkles does, lots of frosting!).

I warmed the butter in the microwave for about 9-10 seconds on HIGH power in a small microwave safe bowl, basically you don't want it softened but not cold either. Just in between the two. Also, alternately you could use unsalted butter and add 1/4 tsp salt to the recipe. I just always keep salted butter on hand so I wanted the recipe to use salted. So if you use salted you don't need to add any salt to the recipe.

Cream Cheese Frosting

In a large mixing bowl, using and electric mixer, whip together butter and cream cheese until pale and fluffy (about 1 minute on high speed, then 3-4 minutes on medium high speed). Mix in vanilla extract. Add powdered sugar and beat until smooth. If doing optional infamous Sprinkles Cupcakes dot on top then scoop out a few tablespoons frosting into two separate bowls and tint with food coloring (lots of red in the one and barely any blue in the other). Spread a small circle of red on top followed by a small light blue, use a toothpick to spread if needed (it helped me get a more circular shape around the edges with its finer point).

Copycat Krispy Kreme Glazed Doughnuts

Active ingredients
Doughnuts
2 1/4 tsp active dry yeast
1/2 cup warm water , 110 degrees
1/4 cup granulated sugar , divided
1/4 cup evaporated milk , warmed to 110 degrees
1/2 tsp salt
1/4 cup vegetable shortening , at room temperature
1 large egg
1 egg yolk
1/2 tsp vanilla extract
2 1/2 cups all-purpose flour , then more as needed
3 - 4 cups vegetable shortening , for frying

Glaze
2 Tbsp unsalted butter , melted
1 1/3 cups powdered sugar
1 pinch salt
2 tsp evaporated milk
1/2 tsp vanilla extract
3 - 4 tsp hot water

Instructions

In the bowl of an electric stand mixer, whisk together yeast, warm water and 1/2 tsp of the sugar. Let rest 5 - 10 minutes. Add in evaporated milk, remaining granulated sugar (3 Tbsp + 2 1/2 tsp), salt, 1/4 cup shortening, egg, egg yolk and vanilla. Add half of the flour and set mixer with whisk attachment and blend until smooth. Switch mixer to hook attachment, slowly add remaining flour and knead on low speed until smooth and elastic about 4 - 5 minutes, adding additional flour as needed (I only added about 2 Tbsp more. You shouldn't need a lot more, you want dough to be slightly sticky and tacky but shouldn't stick to a clean fingertip). Transfer dough to a lightly oiled bowl, cover with plastic wrap and let rise in a warm place until double in size, about 1 1/2 hours.

Punch dough down and roll into an even layer onto a floured surface to slightly less than 1/2-inch thickness. Cut into doughnut shapes using a doughnut cutter or two round circle cutters (on large and one small for holes). Cover and let rise until doubled, about 30 - 40 minutes.

Heat shortening in a cast iron dutch oven to 360 degrees (don't walk away from oil while preheating and don't let it get above 375 degrees, remove from heat and reduce heat as needed). Meanwhile, prepare glaze by mixing together all of the glaze ingredients in a shallow dish (don't add too much water, you'll be dipping warm doughnuts in glaze so you don't want it to be runny, fairly thick is good). Carefully transfer doughnuts to oil (I could fry 3 at a time) and fry until golden on bottom, then using a wooden chopstick, flip to opposite side and fry opposite side until golden brown. Transfer to a wire rack and allow to cool 1 - 2 minutes then dip top half in glaze while still warm and return to wire rack and allow glaze to set at room temperature. Best served warm. Once cool reheat in microwave 5 - 10 seconds if desired.

Halal Cart Chicken and Rice

Active ingredients
Chicken:
¼ cup light olive oil
2 tablespoons lemon juice
1 ½ tablespoons coarsely chopped garlic
1 tablespoon chopped fresh oregano
½ teaspoon ground coriander
kosher salt and ground black pepper to taste
2 pounds boneless chicken thighs, trimmed of excess fat
Yogurt Sauce:
1 cup Greek yogurt
1 tablespoon sriracha sauce, or more to taste
2 cloves garlic, minced
Rice:
2 tablespoons unsalted butter
½ teaspoon ground turmeric
¼ teaspoon ground cumin
1 ½ cups long-grain rice
2 ½ cups chicken broth

Instructions
Combine olive oil, lemon juice, garlic, oregano, and coriander in a blender; blend until smooth. Season with salt and pepper.
Place chicken thighs in a resealable plastic bag; pour in blended marinade and seal. Refrigerate for 3 to 4 hours.
Whisk yogurt, sriracha sauce, garlic, salt, and pepper together to make the sauce. Refrigerate for 1 hour.
Preheat a skillet over medium-high heat. Remove chicken from the marinade and pat dry with paper towels. Cook skin-side down until well browned, 4 to 5 minutes. Flip and cook until no longer pink in the center, 4 to 5 minutes more.
Let chicken for 5 to 10 minutes, then chop into chunks.

Melt butter in a large Dutch oven over medium heat. Add turmeric and cumin; cook and stir until fragrant. Add rice and stir to coat. Cook, stirring frequently, until toasted, about 4 minutes. Pour in chicken broth and season with salt and pepper. Bring to a boil; reduce heat, cover, and cook until broth is absorbed, about 15 minutes.

Remove Dutch oven from the heat and let stand, covered, for 15 minutes.

Divide rice and chicken among serving bowls. Drizzle yogurt sauce on top.

Chef John's Copycat McRib Sandwich

Active ingredients
For the Dry Rub:
1/3 cup kosher salt
1/4 cup brown sugar
2 tablespoons chili powder
2 tablespoons freshly ground black pepper
1 tablespoon ground cumin
1 teaspoon cayenne pepper
For the Sandwiches:
2 racks baby back pork ribs
1 cup barbecue sauce, divided
4 sesame hamburger rolls, split and toasted
1 cup coleslaw

Instructions
Preheat the oven to 325 degrees F (165 degrees C).

Mix salt, brown sugar, chili powder, pepper, cumin, and cayenne together for the rub.

Place ribs on a foil-lined baking sheet. Season both sides generously with some of the rub. Reserve remaining rub for another use. Cover top with parchment paper and wrap foil over the edges. Cover the whole baking sheet with another large sheet of foil, sealing in the sides.

Bake in the preheated oven until tender, about 2 hours and 45 minutes.

Unwrap ribs and let cool briefly until safe to handle. Pull out the bones, stuffing any loose pieces of meat back into the holes and checking carefully for bone fragments. Wrap ribs back up and refrigerate until cold, 8 hours to overnight.

Cut each rack in half. Brush both sides generously with barbecue sauce.

Preheat a charcoal grill for high heat and lightly oil the grate.

Grill ribs until heated through, 3 to 4 minutes per side. Remove from grill and brush with more barbecue sauce.

Drizzle more barbecue sauce onto each roll. Sandwich each rib section between a roll and top with coleslaw.

You might also like

Footnotes

Chef's Notes:

Make sure you don't get the larger St. Louis-style ribs. Feel free to season them with any dry rub of your choice.

For the slaw, I used my sweet-hot mustard coleslaw.

Copycat KFC Coleslaw

Active ingredients
½ small head cabbage, cored and cut into 8 pieces (2 lb)
1 small carrot, cut into 4 pieces
1 tablespoon finely chopped onion
2/3 cup mayonnaise
1/3 cup sugar
1 tablespoon apple cider vinegar
½ teaspoon ground mustard
½ teaspoon salt
Dash paprika

Instructions
Prevent your screen from going dark while you cook.

In 7- to 10-cup food processor, add cabbage; cover, and pulse in short increments until finely chopped. Transfer cabbage to large bowl.

Add carrot to food processor; pulse in short increments until finely chopped. In fine mesh sieve, rinse carrots under cold water until water is clear. Drain carrots thoroughly; add to bowl with cabbage. Stir in onion.

In small bowl, mix remaining ingredients to make dressing. Add to cabbage mixture in bowl; mix well.

Cover and refrigerate at least 1 hour before serving.

Expert Tips
Using your food processor with the S-blade will help give you the smaller, fine chop that is signature to the KFC® coleslaw. For the best results, pulse the vegetables in shorter increments until you get the chop you desire. If you don't have a food processor, you can chop finely using a sharp chef's knife for similar results.

We like to run our carrots under water after they've been chopped to rinse away some of the extra carrot juice that could tint the coleslaw orange.

This coleslaw tastes best when you make it ahead and give it time to sit for a while.
One-half small cabbage finely chopped, should yield 4 cups.
One small carrot finely chopped, should yield about 1/4 cup

Starbucks Iced Peppermint Mochas

Active ingredients
6-7 coffee ice cubes
4 tablespoons sugar (or to taste)
A generous squirt of chocolate syrup (approximately 1/8 cup)
1 tablespoon peppermint syrup
1 cup prepared powdered milk

Instructions
Place all ingredients into the blender and blend until smooth. This will yield one huge mocha or two smaller mochas.

Mocha Frappuccino

Active ingredients
3/4 cup espresso (or double strength coffee)
3/4 cup milk (soy, rice, low fat, 2%, whole, etc)
4 tbsp sugar
3 tbsp unsweetened cocoa powder
pinch of xanthan gum (about 1/16 tsp)
2 cups ice

Instructions
In a large blender add warm coffee, sugar, cocoa powder, and xanthan gum and process on slow speed for about 30 seconds. (The warm coffee helps to dissolve the sugar and completely blended in the xanthan gum.)
Add milk and blend for about 15 seconds just to combine. Finally, add in ice and blend on high power until ice is completely crushed and blended into coffee mixture.
Pour into a large cup and top with whipped cream and a drizzle of chocolate syrup if desired.

NUTRITION
Amount Per Serving: Calories: 305 Total Fat: 4g Saturated Fat: 1g Sodium: 89mg Carbohydrates: 71g Sugar: 54g Protein: 8g

Healthy Starbucks Mocha Frappuccino

Active ingredients
2 cups strong brewed coffee chilled
1/4 cup half and half or almond milk
2 tablespoons cocoa powder
1 tablespoon vanilla extract
14 drops chocolate stevia or sweetener of choice (ie honey,maple syrup, etc.)
1 pinch sea salt
ice
whipped cream and dark chocolate shavings optional garnish

Instructions
Combine coffee, half and half, cocoa powder, vanilla, stevia and salt in a blender. Puree until smooth about 30-60 seconds.
Add a scoop or two of ice and puree for additional 45-60 seconds on high.
Pour into a glass and garnish with whipped cream and dark chocolate shavings.
Chef's Notes:
For a thicker consistency, add more ice.
Stevia has no calories so if you swap with honey or another sweetener please note that the calorie total will increase a bit.

Nutrition
Calories: 72kcal | Carbohydrates: 6.8g | Protein: 2.2g | Fat: 4.2g | Saturated Fat: 2.6g | Polyunsaturated Fat: 1.6g | Cholesterol: 11mg | Sodium: 298mg | Fiber: 1.8g | Sugar: 2g

Mocha cookie frozen coffee

Active ingredients
I full tray of frozen coffee ice cubes coffee brewed then placed in ice cube trays and frozen overnight; affiliate
3/4 or 1 cup milk more or less to taste and consistency
1-2 tbs sugar more or less to taste; affiliate
2 tbs Hershey's Chocolate Syrup affiliate
1/4 cup mini semi-sweet chocolate chips affiliate
1/4 cup crushed Oreo Cookies use with the middle cream part taken out; affiliate
Chocolate whipped cream Beat together 1/4 cup sugar with 2 tbs cocoa [affiliate] and 1 cup whipping cream

Instructions
Blend all ingredient except the chocolate whipped cream in a blender. Blend until smooth. Pour into glass and serve with the chocolate whipped cream and a few sprinkles of the crushed Oreo's. Enjoy!!

Starbucks Iced Caramel Snickers Frappuccino

Active ingredients
1 Snickers Bar or two fun size bars
1/2 cup heavy cream + 2 tablespoons
1 teaspoon vanilla extract
1 tablespoon powdered sugar
1 cup Starbucks Caramel Iced Coffee Beverage
Caramel
1/2 cup ice
caramel-snickers-latte

Instructions
Chop your Snickers Bars into little chunks.
In a stand mixer, mix your vanilla, powdered sugar and cream until soft peaks form
In a blender, combine your ice, and Starbucks Caramel Iced Coffee Beverage; and 2 tablespoons of cream-blended until icy and smooth
Squirt the bottom of your cup with caramel sauce. Pour the icy mixture into your cup. Top with a generous dollop of whopped cream, Snickers, and then drizzle with caramel sauce

Very Berry Hibiscus Tea Refresher

Active ingredients
For the Tea:
8 tea bags of hibiscus berry tea
2 quarts water
1/2 cup berries, fresh or frozen
For the Simple Syrup:
1 cup sugar
1 cup dried hibiscus flowers
2 cups water

Instructions
Make 2 quarts of tea according to package instructions. I brought 2 quarts of water almost to a boil on the stove and then turned off the heat, and added 8 tea bags to infuse (covered) for about 3 minutes.

Take out tea bags and pour tea into a plastic pitcher. Set aside pitcher and let cool to room temperature.

To make the simple syrup, bring water to a boil water with sugar and hibiscus flowers. Turn down heat and simmer for about 20 minutes covered making sure to stir a few times.

Strain leaves and then add syrup to the tea and stir. Refrigerate. Before serving, add berries and about 2 cups of ice. I recommend pouring some tea in a cup with a lid and shaking it up with the berries. Enjoy!

Note: The tea that I used is a Wild Berry Hibiscus by Zhen's Gypsy Tea which I purchased at Cost Plus World Market. I found dried hibiscus flowers at a local organic herbal tea shop. Hibiscus leaves are known to lower cholesterol and blood pressure. Hibiscus has more of a tart flavor so adding some berries and sugar creates more of a subtle sweet flavor.

Copycat Starbucks Strawberries & Creme Frappuccino

Active ingredients
1 cup Milk
2/3 cup Vanilla Ice Cream
1 cup Ice
4-5 Strawberries
1/4 cup Strawberry Syrup /strawberry sauce
1/4 tsp Xanthan Gum optional
Whipped Cream

Instructions
Put all the ingredients other than whipped cream in blender and blend until smooth.
When the fully blended, pour into glasses and top with whipped cream.
Recipe Notes
Xanthan gum is a thickener often used commercial foods, but home cooks are using it more often, especially for gluten free recipes and treats like this Strawberries and cream frap. It can be purchased from Amazon, or your local natural grocer.

Copycat Arby's Sauce

Active ingredients
1/2 cup ketchup
1/2 cup water
2 tablespoons Heinz 57 Steak Sauce
2 teaspoons brown sugar
2 teaspoons white vinegar
1 teaspoon hot sauce
 1/4 teaspoon onion powder
1/4 teaspoon garlic powder
1/4 teaspoon white pepper
1/4 teaspoon kosher salt
1/8 teaspoon black pepper Pinch of nutmeg

Instructions
Whisk together all ingredients in a medium bowl until well blended. Chill until ready to serve. Store in airtight container in refrigerator up to 2 weeks.

Chicken Parm Pockets

Active ingredients
Cooking spray, for baking sheet
1 tube crescent rolls
1/3 c. marinara, plus more for dipping
1 c. mozzarella
1 c. breaded chicken breast, chopped
1/2 c. Parmesan
6 Basil Leaves, Torn
1 tbsp. Italian seasoning
1 egg, for eggwash
Cold water, for eggwash

Instructions
Preheat oven to 375° and grease a large baking sheet with cooking spray.

Roll out crescent dough, divide into rectangles, and pinch perforations to seal. Top one side of each rectangle with 1 tbsp. marinara sauce, 1 tbsp. mozzarella, 2 tbsp. breaded chicken, 1 tbsp. parmesan, and 1 torn basil leaf. Sprinkle with more mozzarella and a pinch of Italian seasoning, then fold opposite side over and pinch sides to seal. Repeat with remaining rectangles.

Brush each pocket with 1 tbsp. egg wash and sprinkle with more Italian seasoning.

Bake until pockets are golden and cheese is melty, 18-20 minutes. Let cool and serve with marinara for dipping.

Broccoli-Cheddar Homemade "Hot Pockets"

Active ingredients
1 lb. store-bought or homemade pie crust
1 c. shredded Cheddar
2 c. cooked broccoli florets, chopped
1/2 lb. ham, chopped
1 large egg, beaten with 1 tbsp. water

Instructions
Preheat oven to 350 degrees F and line a baking sheet with parchment paper. On a floured work surface, roll out pie dough into a rectangle and slice off rounded edges (if using store-bought).
Cut into four strips and top the bottom halves of each strip with cheddar, broccoli, and ham.
Fold over top half of strip and seal by pinching crust with your fingers. Use the twine of a fork to crimp. Brush with egg wash and transfer to prepared baking sheet.
Bake until golden and puffy, 18 to 20 minutes

Chicken Pot Pie Homemade "Hot Pockets"

Active ingredients
1 lb. store-bought or homemade pie crust
3/4 lb. boneless skinless chicken breast, cooked
2 c. mixed frozen vegetables, thawed
1/4 c. all-purpose flour
1/2 c. whole milk
kosher salt
Freshly ground black pepper
1 large egg, beaten with 1 tbsp. water

Instructions
Preheat oven to 350 degrees F and line a baking sheet with parchment paper. On a floured work surface, roll out pie crust into a large rectangle and slice off rounded edges (if using store-bought). Slice into four strips.

Place cooked chicken and vegetables in a large mixing bowl. In a small saucepan over low heat, whisk flour and milk and let simmer, 5 minutes until thick. Pour sauce over chicken and vegetables and season generously with salt and pepper.

Spoon mixture over bottom halves of pie crust strips and fold over tops.

Use your fingers to pinch to seal and press the twines of a fork to crimp. Brush with egg wash and transfer to prepared baking sheet.

Bake until golden and puffy, 18 to 20 minutes.

Pizza Homemade "Hot Pockets"

Active ingredients
1 lb. store-bought or homemade pie crust
1/2 c. marinara
1 1/2 c. shredded mozzarella
1/2 c. mini pepperoni
1 large egg, beaten with 1 tbsp. water

Instructions
Preheat oven to 350 degrees F and line a baking sheet with parchment paper. On a floured work surface, roll out pie crust into a large rectangle and slice off rounded edges (if using store-bought). Slice into four strips.

Spoon marinara over bottom half of strips and top with mozzarella and pepperoni. Fold over tops.

Use your fingers to pinch to seal and press the twines of a fork to crimp. Brush with egg wash and transfer to prepared baking sheet.

Bake until golden and puffy, 18 to 20 minutes.

Meatball Sub "Hot Pockets"

Active ingredients
1 lb. lean ground beef
1/2 c. Italian bread crumbs
2 cloves garlic, minced
1/4 c. fresh Italian parsley
1 tsp. crushed red pepper flakes
kosher salt
Freshly ground black pepper
1 lb. store-bought or refrigerated pie crust
1/2 c. marinara
1 1/2 c. mozzarella
1 large egg, beaten with 1 tbsp. water

Instructions
Preheat oven to 350° and line two baking sheet with parchment paper. Make mini meatballs: In a large bowl, combine ground beef, bread crumbs, garlic, parsley, and crushed red pepper flakes and season with salt and pepper. Roll into meatballs and transfer to one prepared baking sheet. Bake until browned and cooked through, 15 minutes.
On a floured work surface, roll out pie crust into a large rectangle and slice off rounded edges (if using store-bought). Slice into four strips.

Spoon marinara, meatballs, and mozzarella onto bottom halves of pie crust strips and fold over tops.

Use your fingers to pinch to seal and press the twines of a fork to crimp. Brush with egg wash and transfer to prepared baking sheet.

Bake until golden and puffy, 18 to 20 minutes.

Egg, Avocado, and Cheddar Homemade "Hot Pockets"

Active ingredients
1 lb. store-bought or refrigerated pie crust
6 large eggs, well beaten
kosher salt
Freshly ground black pepper
1 avocado, mashed
1 c. shredded Cheddar

Instructions
Preheat oven to 350 degrees F and line a baking sheet with parchment paper. On a floured work surface, roll out pie crust into a large rectangle and slice off rounded edges (if using store-bought). Slice into four strips.

In a large nonstick skillet, pour in beaten eggs, season with salt and pepper, and scramble, 3 minutes. Spoon over bottom halves of pie crust. Top with avocado and cheddar and fold over tops.

Use your fingers to pinch to seal and press the twines of a fork to crimp. Brush with egg wash and transfer to prepared baking sheet.

Bake until golden and puffy, 18 to 20 minutes.

Skyline Lentil Chili

Active ingredients
Seasoning Mix:
2 tablespoons chili powder, or more to taste
2 teaspoons garlic powder
1/2 (1 ounce) square unsweetened chocolate, grated
1 teaspoon ground cinnamon
1 teaspoon ground cumin
1/2 teaspoon salt
1/2 teaspoon cayenne pepper
1/4 teaspoon ground allspice
1/4 teaspoon ground cloves
1 bay leaf
Lentil Chili:
1 tablespoon olive oil, or as needed
2 cups diced onions
2 cups diced green bell pepper
6 cups vegetable broth
2 cups dry lentils
2 (8 ounce) cans tomato sauce
2 tablespoons apple cider vinegar
2 teaspoons Worcestershire sauce
1/2 cup water, or as needed (optional)

Instructions
Mix chili powder, garlic powder, unsweetened chocolate, cinnamon, cumin, salt, cayenne pepper, allspice, cloves, and bay leaf together in a bowl until seasoning mix is well combined.

Heat olive oil in a Dutch oven over medium heat; cook and stir onions and green bell pepper until lightly browned, about 10 minutes. Add vegetable broth and lentils; simmer for 20 minutes. Stir in seasoning mix, tomato sauce, apple cider vinegar, and Worcestershire sauce; simmer for 1 hour more, adding water if chili gets too thick.

Remove bay leaf from chili. Blend chili using an immersion blender until desired consistency is reached.

Cooking for one

Today, more and more of us live alone, either through choice or circumstances. But the great thing about cooking for one is that you don't have to please anyone but yourself. Cook using the ingredients you enjoy, even if they're not to other people's liking, or have breakfast for dinner if that's what you feel like.

Cooking for one doesn't mean cooking or eating alone
Cooking at home doesn't have to mean spending more time alone. You can make your own healthy meals and still find that social connection we all crave.

Cook a little extra and invite a coworker or neighbor to join you. Or take turns preparing meals for each other.
Make your food at home, then eat out at the park, picnic area, museum, food court, or coffee shop. Having enough food to share with others can be a great way to break the ice and make new friends.
Shop for food at a farmer's market instead of a grocery store. People here are more likely to take time to discuss the food and give cooking tips, making it easier to strike up new friendships.
If you don't have people in your life that you want to eat with, find ways to meet new people. Take a cooking class, join a club, or enroll in a special interest group that meets on a regular basis. Volunteering is another great way to find future dining companions.

Cooking without a real kitchen

Whether you have a full kitchen, a sluggish cooker and devices like a cleaner and toaster oven can be quicker and simpler to utilize, specifically if you're an amateur cook.

Toaster. Due to the fact that it heats up quickly, a toaster oven is an affordable method to broil, bake, roast veggies, or make toasted sandwiches.

Hot plate. Ideal for hotel rooms, dormitory spaces, and little homes. Almost anything that can be made on a stove top can be made on a hot plate with a pan or fry pan.

Rice cooker. With a little creativity, it can also be utilized to cook delicious one-pot meals along with rice.

Cleaner. Steaming is one of the quickest and healthiest ways to prepare food. You can use a standalone electronic steamer or a steamer basket that fits into a saucepan.

Steamed veggies do not have to be dull
Steamed vegetables such as broccoli, Brussels sprouts, green beans, carrots, and asparagus can be tasty as well as quick and nutritious.

Steam very finely sliced veggies. For a flavor increase, include stock to the water.
Top with olive oil, herbs, or with a healthy and fast sauce.
Include fish, thin strips of chicken, or tofu for a total meal.

CONCLUSION

If you are a food-driven soul, having a really good meal is one of the great pleasures of life. Such a reward may be even the administrative labor of dining out— making a reservation, getting ready and, of course, settling down to order. But the most magical moment of all is when the long-awaited food arrives– gliding through a crowed dining room and ready to be enjoyed before being put on the table. Including beautifully designed salads and incredibly well crispy, delicious fried allthings to silky spaghetti and perfectly cooked steaks— good food for the restaurants always seems to have a little extra to make it show.

But if you've ever badly prepared food of this kind on your own, there is hope! With just a few simple tricks and tips, you can also cook quality cuisine in your own kitchen. These are tricks that may not seem so strong on their own, but can transform how you prepare and produce food when they are all used together. These tips help you cook at home like a pro from expired spices and how you use salt to literally arrange it before you start cooking.

Disclaimer

This book is not intended as a substitute for the medical advice of physicians. The reader should regularly consult a physician in matters relating to his/her health and particularly with respect to any symptoms that may require diagnosis or medical attention.

Do Not Go Yet; One Last Thing To Do
If you enjoyed this book or found it useful, I'd be very grateful if you'd post a short review on Amazon. Your support does make a difference, and I read all the reviews personally so I can get your feedback and make this book even better.
Thanks again for your support!

Lightning Source UK Ltd.
Milton Keynes UK
UKHW020630081220
374827UK00013B/1083

9 781914 120053